Rs 200/-
1
AF651464

PSYCHOLOGY OF READING
Role of Orthographic Features

Advances in Psychological Research in India Series

1. Perspectives on Psychology and Social Development
   U.N. Dash and **Uday Jain** (Ed)
2. Psychology of Poverty and Disadvantage
   Ajit K. Mohanty and **Girishwar Misra** (Eds)
3. Perspective on Indigenous Psychology
   Girishwar Misra and **Ajit K. Mohanty**
4. Psychology of Reading: Role of Orthographic Features
   Shantilata Sahu
5. Personality: Issues in Assessment and Projective Inventory Approach **P.K. Rath**

About the Author

The author of this book Dr. (Mrs.) **Shantilata Sahu,** did her M.A. and Ph.D. in Psychology from Utkal University. Having a bright career to her credit, she was also a recipient of Commonwealth Scholarship, Commonwealth Post-Doctoral Fellowship, and USEFI Visiting Fellowship. She has been declared as an Associate of Institute of Education, University of London, in recognition of her studies at the Institute. She has published in different national and international journals, and has presented papers in conferences, symposia and seminars. She has authored another book entitled *Learning to Read: Use of Orthographic and Context Cues.* Her research interests include Psycholinguistics, Cognition, and Education. At present she is working as a Professor, in the Centre of Advance Study in Psychology, Utkal University.

About the Institution

The Centre of Advance Study in Psychology, Utkal University, is the first such Centre for Psychology in India. The Centre specialise in broad areas of Educational and Developmental Psychology. Social and Organizational Psychology as well as Comparative and Physiological Psychology, Members of its faculty, one of the largest among the university departments of Psychology in India, are highly qualified and internationally reputed for their contributions in various fields of research and applications, in Social psychology, cognitive development, information processing early childhood education, psycholinguistics, testing and measurement and exploratory behaviour. The Centre which has a large number of acclaimed publications to its credit, has currently launched a publication series 'Advances in Psychological Research in India.' Its teaching programme includes, Diploma in Early Childhood Education, besides Masters, M.Phil and Doctoral work in Psychology.

Advances in Psychological Research in India Series—4

PSYCHOLOGY OF READING

Role of Orthographic Features

SHANTILATA SAHU
Centre of Advance Study in Psychology
Utkal University

CONCEPT PUBLISHING COMPANY, NEW DELHI - 110059

All rights reserved. No part of this work may be reproduced, stored in a retrieval system, or transmitted in any form or by any means, electronic, mechanical, photocopying, recording or otherwise, without the prior written permission of the copyright owner and the publisher.

ISBN 81- 7022-832-8

First Published 2000

© Centre of Advance Study in Psychology,
Utkal University, Bhubaneswar.

Published and Printed by

Ashok Kumar Mittal
Concept Publishing Company
A /15 -16, Commercial Block, Mohan Garden,
New Delhi - 110059 (India)

Phones: 5648039, 5649024

Fax: 091-11-5648053

E-mail: publishing@conceptpub.com

to

my students

who have worked with me

PREFACE

What is reading? Definitely it is not identifying the individual letters, putting them together and then locating the word; and continuing in this way till we finish a sentence. Then, starting the same process with the next sentence till we finish a paragraph. Again, repeating the whole thing till we end a write-up. Had it been this, then reading time, for example, for a word would have been equal to the sum total of letter identification time for all the letters contained in the word. But, it is not. Reading time happens to be much lesser than that. Besides, had we been proceeding in the above way, could we end up in understanding a write-up? That is, could we ever attain "comprehension"? Most likely not. If reading is not letter-by-letter identification, then what it is? Such quastions bother most of us. Probably reading is not letter-by-letter identification only though it starts with in-puts from them. It involves some other processes, is influenced by some variables, some factors. What these processes, variables or factors could be?

Besides, why is it that children are slow and jerky at reading? Their understanding of written texts are also poor. How mastery in reading is achieved? Probably beginning reading and fluent reading basically involve different processes and, hence, are basically different from each other.

Reading researchers, mostly in the context of English writing system, are plenty in number. Such researches in Chinese, Japanese, French, and other writing systems have also been done. Are the findings available in these orthographies universal? What could be the contribution of a specific orthography to its reading processes?

Such considerations propelled us to conduct researches reported in this volume. Some of these researches were reported in some journals. Publications in pieces fail to make much meaning. So, selected publications and some unpublished research reports till date have been put together in this volume, so that they may make some meaning. The volume reports of studies done to see beginning reading processes, lexical access processes, and cognitive correlates/determiners of reading. Attempts have been made to locate orthographic universalities and specificities.

We will deem our efforts effective if this volume makes any meaningful contribution in locating orthography-universalities and/or specificities in reading processes.

SHANTILATA SAHU

ACKNOWLEDGEMENTS

This is an occasion to express my gratitude to those for whom this monograph has been a possibility. First and foremost, I thank children who agreed and participated in different studies. I thank their school authorities for giving me permission to conduct my studies. My students have helped me in many ways—they deserve special mention here. The Co-ordinator of Centre of Advance Studies in Psychology at Utkal, Prof. A. K. Mohanty has taken keen interest in publishing this work. His suggestions for modification have helped me a lot. Also, he has put in much efforts to see this book out. I herewith express my sincere thanks to him. The Head of my Department Dr. Banamali Mohanty has encouraged me to bring out this volume. I acknowledge his colleague—like support. Some of the studies put in this monograph were published in *Journal of Research in Reading,* United Kingdom Reading Association, U.K., *Journal of Psychological Researches,* Madras; *Psycho-Lingua,* Agra; and *Indian Journal of Adult Education,* New Delhi. I thank the Editors of these journals for permitting me to report them in this volume. Concept Publishing Company, New Delhi has taken up the job of publishing it. Thanks to their efforts.

Last, but not the least, my typist, Sri. S.N.Behera did the job of typing the manuscript. He has done it neatly—thanks to him.

Without a single person's help and interest mentioned above this monograph would not have been a possibility. My gratitude to all of them.

SHANTILATA SAHU

CONTENTS

LIST OF TABLES

LIST OF FIGURES

PROLOGUE

Reading and its Facets

So far as the term 'reading' is concerned we get varied expressions like- 'I could not read his mind'; or 'it is difficult to take a reading of weather'; or 'he is very fluent at reading'. In all these sentences the speaker refers to some 'reading' process. In the first sentence the speaker says that he could not make out what the other person was thinking; in the second the speaker says that he was not able to predict the weather; and in the third the speaker means that the other person was very efficient in reading a written text. One commonality about 'reading' that emerges out is, *reading refers to making out a meaning;* whether it is about the intentions of someone, or about predictions relating to weather; or about understanding a written text.

The reader always tries to make out a meaning, but out of what?– out of a complex set of stimuli. A complex set of stimuli lie in front of him and he grapples through it in order to get a sense, a meaning. Reading refers to making out a meaning out of a stimulus complex.

The present book deals with text reading processes. So far as text reading is concerned it could be viewed to be a process of arriving at a meaning out of what is there in a given text. The text contains visual information, linguistic information, including semantic information, and syntactic information. Besides, the text could also be mapped into phonetic spaces. The reader also himself brings with him a whole backdrop of world knowledge and experience. Thus, in a reading situation there is an interaction between all these information against the reader's backdrop. *Text reading is skimming or scanning through all these stimuli against reader's backdrop of knowledge while striving to arrive at a meaning.*

While scanning the stimulus complex the reader selects significant bits/dimensions of the stimulus complex instead of taking note of all the bits of information into account. *Reading involves selectivity.*

So far as reading processes and its facets are concerned, it could be broadly viewed to be consisting of oral reading, silent reading, and reading comprehension processes. Oral reading is reading aloud a text and thus is basically concerned with letter-to-sound mapping. On the other hand, reading comprehension is concerned with getting at the meaning of the text irrespective of reading the text loudly or silently. It involves processing of bits of information contained in a given text. Comprehension draws on the reader's world knowledge, past experience and language competence. Comprehension may involve any one of the following processes. Comprehension may aim at arriving at the given bits of information. This refers to *literal comprehension.* On the other hand some times comprehension may aim at going beyond the bits of information given in a text i.e., inferencing on the bases of the given information. This is *inferential comprehension.* This could be viewed to be a 'reading between lines' process since it involves reasoning and inferencing processes.

Researchers view that oral reading and reading comprehension may or may not go together. Sometimes oral reading is plain and simple conversion of graphemes to phonetic sounds devoid of getting at the meaning of what is read. Such a reading is known as 'barking at words' or 'word calling'. On the other hand, sometimes oral reading goes hand in hand with getting at the meaning of what is being read; hence involves comprehension. However, whether oral reading will go with comprehension or not depends upon the level of reading skill of the reader, his purpose of reading and the difficulty level of the text.

Orthographies

Writing systems or orthographies vary widely from each other. Orthographic patterns can be broadly divided into logographic, syllabic, and alphabetic types. The logographic writing system involves pictorial way of depiction. Syllabic orthographies involve characters, which are syllables. Alphabetic orthographies involve alphebets as characters and each alphabet stands for a segment of a speech sound i.e., a phoneme. Hence, single alphabets are not pronounceable as such. Combinations of alphabets make up pronounceable units.

Another way of categorizing orthographies is dividing them into phonemic or non-phonemic types. A phonemic orthography is one where each character stands for a phoneme. On the other hand, a non-phonemic orthography is one where characters do not stand for phonemes. This division is like dividing orthographies into alphabetic and non-alphabetic types.

Besides, orthographies can be divided into phonetic and non-phonetic types. A phonetic orthography has almost invariant grapheme-to-phoneme correspondence, whereas a non-phonetic orthography has varying grapheme-to-phoneme correspondences. In the former type letters retain their phonetic sounds accross their uses in various word contexts; but in later case the phonetic sound of a letter depends upon the word context in which it appears; hence varies in different words.

Writing systems in use rarely present 'pure' orthographies in the sense that, they do not contain absolute feature of one or another orthography. Most of the orthographies in use have combinations of different features. They are categorised into different types on the basis/bases of their prominent feature(s).

Oriya Orthography and Reading

Oriya writing system involves 47 characters out of which 35 are consonants and 12 are vowels. Each letter has a fixed phonic sound and this phonic sound is the name of the letter. Each letter is a syllable. The phonic mapping of any letter remains almost the same accross all uses of the letter in all word contexts. Thus grapheme-to-phoneme correspondence is almost invariant in this writing system. Viewing from this context Oriya orthography could be categorised as a syllabic and phonetic type of orthography. So far as the nature of Oriya orthography is concerned its present conceptualization is given in Sahu, Mohanty and Singh's paper (last paper) of this monograph. This paper also presents detailed discussion about the implications of this type of orthography for reading strategies and processes.

This monograph presents some research findings relating to reading processes in the context of Oriya orthography. Contents have been broadly divided into three sections: beginning reading; lexical access; and cognitive correlates/determiners. In the first section findings relating to beginning reading accross two different orthographies and developmental changes in oral reading strategies of Oriya readers have been presented. Second section deals with lexical access modes for readers reading in Oriya orthography. Third section presents findings relating to cognitive correlates/determiners of reading in Oriya orthography.

SECTION -I

BEGINNING READING

1

LEARNING TO READ
Observations Across Two Orthographies

Reading is decoding from print. It could be broadly divided into two categories: oral reading; and reading with comprehension. Oral reading primarily involves decoding the written symbols into vocal sound patterns i.e. print-to-sound conversion with or without comprehension of the written text. On the other hand, reading comprehension is primarily involved with deciphering the meaning from the text with or without reading aloud the text. The present chapter is concerned with oral reading.

So far as the written symbols are concerned, writing systems or orthographies can be broadly divided into three categories: alphabatic, syllabic and logographic types of orthographies (Taylor, 1981; Varshney, 1988).

Alphabatic writing is one in which graphemes correspond to phonemes. Syllabic writing system is one in which graphmes correspond to syllables. And, a logographic or ideographic writing system is one in which each grapheme stands for a word or morpheme. English, Japanese and Chinese orthographies are examples of alphabatic, syllabic and logographic types of orthographies respectively.

Apart from this, taking into account if letters in an orthography represent speech sounds, orthographies could be divided into phonetic and non-phonetic orthographies (Wagner & Torgesen, 1987). An orthography with poor grapheme-to-phonic correspondence is viewed as a non-phonetic orthography; and an orthography with good grapheme-to-phoneme correspondence is viewed as a phonetic orthography. Thus, orthographies could be either alphabatic, syllabic or logographic types being phonetic or non-phonetic in nature.

Researchers in beginning reading are mostly concerned with what children learn when they learn to read. Juola, Schadler, Chabot,

McCaughey & Wait (1979) in the chapter: "What do children learn when they learn to read?" point out that learning to read basically implies learning of orthographic rules of language, and when a child is learning to read he is basically developing visual processing skills that make use of orthographic regularities; the visual processing skills that help direct recognition of frequently occurring letter clusters and words as perceptual units. Their obervation of visual search strategies of kindergarten, first, second-grade and older children for words, pseudowords and non-words showed that the kindergarteners as different from other groups, not only showed a slow visual scanning rate but also showed a letter-by-letter scanning strategy and did not show differential scanning rates for words, pseudowords and non-words. This observation made them conclude that learning to read means developing an effective visual scanning process involving orthographic rules and regularities for rapid word indentification as perceptual units.

Massaro & Hestand (1983) made first, second and third grade readers pick up nonsense letter strings that looked like words. These letter strings either confirmed to the rules of English writing system or violated these rules (e.g. movule *vs.* plgued; hemort *vs.* cdrtei etc.). Children picked up letter strings that confirmed English writing rule, and this performance imporved with school experience. This observation led authors to conclude that children possess the knowledge of orthographic structures which improves with increasing reading experience. Reading ability was found to be positively correlated with the child's knowledge of orthographic rules.

Francis (1984) opines that children possess the knowledge of spelling; and children's knowledge of spelling of words is shown up in miscue-target orthographic similarity. On the basis of such an orthographic similarity index she advocates for the presence of implicit knowledge of spelling even among beginning readers. This knowledge of spelling, she views, is the result of the child's own information about the individual word and his experience of regularities in spelling across words he has seen and learned to read aloud. Reitsma (1983) even advocates that this knowledge of spelling is well differentiated to the extent of being word-specific among Dutch children.

The present chapter is concerned with the oral reading strategies of beginning readers reading two different orthographies. Since in different orthographies, graphemes correspond to either phonemes or syllables or morphemes or words; and different orthographies are either phonetic or non-phonetic, orthographic variation might be contributing to the reader's reading strategy. Reading strategy, in the present chapter, refers to the selectivity and sampling of visual cues from the print. Precisely, this chapter addresses itself to word identification in sentence context by beginning readers reading two different orthographies.

Method

Subjects

Subjects (*S*s) were English and Oriya beginning readers who read orthographies of their home language. The English reading group consisted of English children and children of immigrant parents in England, all having English as their home language. All these children were drawn from an ILEA (Inner London Education Authority) School of London. These children were either in the first or second year of their school. There were 36 *S*s (17 boys and 19 girls) in the English reading group with a mean age of 6 years 5 months. The Oriya reading group consisted of Oriya children having Oriya as their home language. They were drawn from two High Schools of Bhubaneswar, Orissa. There were 100 *S*s (50 boys and 50 girls) in this group with a mean age of 7 years 1 month. These children were in the second year of their school.

Oral Reading Tasks

English oral reading task

The ILEA school in which the study was done followed the break through method of teaching reading to beginning readers. They started with break-through sentence makers then proceeded to word makers. Look-and-say method was followed at the initial stage, then phonics was being introduced. The children were on a banded reading scheme. A total of seven sentences were used in the present study. These sentences were prepared using a pool of 28 words common to all the *S*s. All children tested on this task were able to make an attempt to read the material (i.e. at least 18 per cent of the total words were read correctly), but none did it perfectly. *S*s were tested individually and were asked to read aloud the sentences. All the responses including correct responses, mis-readings, and no response were recorded. Each *S* was allowed enough time to complete the task. A copy of this task and some examples of children's mis-readings are given in Appendix-I.

Oriya oral reading task

The textbook for the schools of Orissa have been nationalised. Hence, all students of a particular grade are exposed to the same set of books irrespective of their place of schooling in Orissa. So, all the children of grade-I are exposed to one set of language textbooks. The present oral reading task consisted of 29 sentences drawn randomly from the language text book of grade-I. One hundred and thirty-one words made up these 29 sentences. While drawing these sentences from language textbooks of grade-I, care was taken to see that all sorts of spelling variations introduced in the text are included in the reading task. A pilot testing showed that performance on this task correlated significantly ($r = .7258$; $df = 28$; $p < .01$) with teachers' rating of child's reading ability and also with classroom language examination marks ($r = .5558$; $df = 28$; $p < .01$) (Sahu & Patnaik, 1987). Thus it was accepted that this oral reading task was fairly dependable. Each child was tested individually and was asked to read aloud the sentences. Enough time was allowed to complete the task. All responses including correct responses, misreadings, failure to read, omission of words, and addition of words during reading were being recorded.

Results

The study analysed the misreadings (miscues) produced by the *S*s for their orthographic similarity with target words. Miscue-target orthographic similarity for letters in specific positions; and irrespective of their positions were analysed. Table 1.1 presents the orthographic similarity indices in terms of proportions for miscues produced by the English reading sample.

TABLE 1.1: Proportions of miscue-target orthographic similarity indices for miscues produced by English reading groups

	Initial Position	End Position	Mid Position	Regardless of Position
Present data	.559	.283	.271	.510
Francis' (1984) data	.35	.16 (.22 dissregarding word length)	.20	—

Francis (1984) collected miscues from oral reading of children with reading-age ranging from 5 years to 7 years. Miscue—target letter similarity analyses revealed increasing similarity with increasing reading-age (high degree miscue—target similarity or near identity means almost perfect reading with residual errors contributed by context factors). Overall weighted means for all these children of Francis' study is given in the second row of Table 1.1. The present study reveals highest similarity index for initial letter position, followed by letters irespective of their positions, followed by that of the end position. Francis' data corroborates the present observation for initial letter position, and also for end letter position.

Table 1.2 presents the comparable miscue-target orthographic similarity indices of the miscues produced by the Oriya reading group (first row). The second, third and fourth rows present comparable statistics from other data collected from other groups of beginning and fluent (i.e. children drawn from grade-V) readers. Mishras' (1987) data was based on random sample testing of socially advantaged and disadvantaged children. Socially advantaged children were drawn from high caste, high income and high education families and socially disadvantaged children were drawn from low caste, low income and low education families. Socially advantaged children were relatively better readers than socially disadvantaged children.

TABLE: 1.2: Proportions of miscue-target orthographic similarity indices for miscues Produced by Oriya reading groups

	Initial Position	End Position	Mid Position	Regardless of position
Present data				
(beginning readers)	.527	.522	.544	.563
Other Data				
Sahu & Patnaik's	.817 (adv.)	.601 (adv.)	.579 (adv.)	.713 (adv.)
(1987) data	to	to	to	to
(beginning readers)	.780 (dis.)	.591 (dis.)	.650 (dis.)	.714 (dis.)
Mishra's (1987) data	.674	.584	.564	.629
(fluent readers)				
Sahu & Patnaik's	.874 (adv.)	.721 (adv.)	.767 (adv.)	.843 (adv.)
(1987) data	to	to	to	to
(fluent readers)	.838 (dis.)	.695 (dis.)	.664 (dis.)	.751 (dis.)

Abbreviations : adv.-- Socially advantaged

dis. --Socially disadvantaged

Comparison of proportions within each row reflect highest similarity index for initial letter position; then all the letters disregrading their ordinal positions; followed by that of the end letter. The hierarchy of miscue-target orthographic similarity indices projected by all the groups is: initial, total and end positions.

Discussion and Conclusion

The information collected from beginning English readers as well as from beginning and fluent Oriya readers go to substantiate the following facts:

(1) Children, even the beginning reading group, probably have a visual impression of written words;

(2) The impact of initial and end letter positions are prominent in this impression; and

(3) This impression is an overall impression of the word, not a differentiated word-specific letter-by-letter visual image of the word.

Focusing on the beginning reading group first, observation across orthographies show that the beginning English and Oriya reading groups inspite of being either first or second graders in schools, i.e. having very little or about a year's reading instruction, do project a considerable degree of miscue-target orthographic similarity. If this similarity is accepted as an indicator of children's knowledge of spelling, the present study shows that even these children possess a knowledge of spelling of different familiar words.

More experienced readers project a higher degree of similarity between their miscues and the respective target words. Francis' data in Table 1.1 and other data in Table 1.2 confirm this.

In this visual impression of written words letters in different positions carry differential weightage. The initial letter of the word carries the greatest significance, then comes the letter in end position.

The fact that all the letters taken together, irrespective of their positions, also project a high similarity index probably implies that this visual impression is not a word-specific letter-to-letter image of the word. Rather it is an overall generalised global impression of the written word.

How this visual impression develops ? Francis (1984) says this is the result of child's own impression about the word and his experience of regularities in spelling across words he has seen and read. Ehri (1980) says it develops out of visual contact with written words.

Indirect observations of visual scanning of words, pseudo-words, and non-words involving groups of beginning readers and making them pick up non-sense letter strings which look like words, while these letter strings either confirmed to spelling rules or violated them, showed that children possess the knowledge of spelling. Now, if misreading-target orthographic similarity is accepted as a direct evidence of this knowledge, readers both beginning and relatively fluent, reading alphabatic non-phonetic and alphabatic-syllabic-phonetic orthographies reveal having the knowledge of spelling in their own orthographies.

It is pertinent to mention that it would have been ideal had the cultural variance, which goes with general literacy level, been kept constant. That would have allowed drawing a firm conclusion from the observations made. However, the purpose of making readers read orthographies of their home language necessitated the cultural variance.

Summary

Two groups of children learning to read, read aloud sentences written in their home language. Two orthographies involved were: an alphabatic non-phonetic orthography; and an alphabatic-syllabic type of phonetic orthography. Miscue-target similarity indices by letter positions showed highest similarity for initial letters, followed by end letters. Similarity, irrespective of letter positions was also very high. These observations alongwith observations from other data go to show that children, even beginning readers possess knowledge of spelling.

APPENDIX -I

English Oral Reading Task

1. here I am
2. the baby can play
3. here is a big car
4. I can run and jump
5. a boy is in my little house
6. I can go with my mum to the shop
7. dad and mum like my cat and my dog

Examples of children's misreadings

1. boy for baby
2. play for jump
3. big for boy
4. like for little
5. he for house
6. big for dog

Examples of failure to read

little, house, baby, play.

2

DEVELOPMENTAL CHANGES IN ORAL READING STRATEGIES OF ORIYA READERS

Reading has been differently defined by different researchers. Some researchers equate it with phonetic decoding; and some others emphasise that the process of reading is incomplete without arriving at the meaning of the text. However, functionally, reading can be said to be the ability to extract selected visual information from the print and to comprehend its meaning.

While reading, though a reader intends to comprehend the text, yet, sometimes he fails arriving at it. In the later case the reader is a word-caller; giving just a phonetic equivalent of the graphemic input without any understanding. Viewed from this perspective reading processes can be viewed to be involving two clear facets: oral reading and reading comprehension. Danks and Fears (1979) view that oral reading may or may not involve comprehension; depending upon the level of reading skill of the reader and his intentions behind reading.

However, so far as reading process is concerned, it makes use of two major cues; the visual cue and the context cue (Francis, 1982, 1984; Sahu, 1985; Beardsley, 1982). Visual cue consists of the orthographic input from the print; and context cue consists of the semantic and syntactic formulations. So far as visual cues are concerned Francis' (1984) observation in English orthography points out that the initial and end letters are of utmost importance; and with development in reading skill acquisition the use of visual orthographic cues during reading increases. So far as semantic and syntactic cues are concerned similar observations in English orthography point out that their use during reading also shows increment with improving reading proficiency (Beardsley,

---

Co-author Sabita Mishra

1982; Murray and Maliphant, 1982).

Though both graphemic cues and context cues play important roles in reading, yet, their relative use depends on the level of reader's reading competence. The less competent a reader is, the more is his relative dependence on graphemic cues; and the more competent a reader is, the more is his relative dependence on context cues.

It has been observed that orthographic variations may have significant implications for reading success among its readers (Stevenson, Stigler, Lucker, Hsu and Kitamura, 1982). Besides, orthographic variations might be bearing implications for its readers' reading strategies; and might be making different cognitive demands on its readers. So far as types of orthographies are concerned orthographies can be broadly devided into alphabetic, syllabic and logographic types (Taylor, 1981; Varshney, 1985; Reyner and Pollatsek, 1989). And, on the basis of their variance or invariance in grapheme-to-phonic conversion they can be categorised into non-phonetic or phonetic orthographies (Wagner and Torgesen, 1987). Phonemic orthographies are different from phonetic orthographies in the sense that in the former case letters stand for phonemes and in the latter case they stand for speech sounds (Sgall, 1987; Wagner and Torgesen, 1987).

Most of the researches in the field of psychology of reading have been done in the context of English orthography, which is an alphabetic and non-phonetic orthography. Because of its very nature this orthography might be demanding a specific reading strategy, hence, findings in the context of this orthography may not hold good for orthographies which are basically different from this.

Oriya orthography is a syllabic and phonetic type of orthography. Here, each letter is a pronounceable unit; and letter-to-sound correspondence remains almost invariant across all its usage. This orthography probably demands a reading strategy significantly different from one involved in reading English orthography.

The present study aimed to look into the oral reading strategies of beginning Oriya readers and the possible developmental changes in it.

Method

Design

The present study included children from grades II and V. Grade II represents the stage of beginning reading when children start learning how to read a text. Grade V represents the final stage in primary schooling; and by this stage children presumably have mastery over oral reading; and are expected to be fluent oral readers. Fifty *S*s (subjects) from each grade, with equal number of boys and girls were drawn randomly to serve as *S*s for the present study. Thus the design was a 2x2 factorial design (i.e. 2 levels of grade being orthogonally combined into 2 sex groups); with N = 25 in each cell. All these *S*s were administered with grade-appropriate oral reading tasks.

Subjects

Subjects for the present study were drawn from one of the schools of Bhubaneswar, the capital city of Orissa. This school followed the syllabus and text books prescribed by the Government of Orissa; and the medium of instruction in this school was Oriya, the mother tongue of the present sample.

Procedure of Data Collection

Sahu and Patnaik's (1987) grade—appropriate oral reading tasks were administered on the present sample. This task for grade-II consists of 29 sentences and that for grade-V consists of 34 sentences. The *S* is given a chart containing all these sentences and he is asked to read aloud the sentences. As the *S* reads, the experimenter *(E)* records *S*'s reading performance in a response record sheet. Words correctly read; words that are attempted to be read but are read incorrectly (i.e. miscues); words that were attempted to be read but could not be read at all (i.e. failures); words that were omitted; and words that were added during reading were being recorded. Reading task was individually administered on all *S*s. There was no time limit to complete the task. Besides oral reading performance each *S*'s age record, as on the date of testing, was noted down.

Results

It was found that on the whole boys and girls of a given grade did not differ significantly. Hence, scores for the two sex groups were pooled together and $\overline{X}$s and SDs were obtained for the total samples of each grade. These $\overline{X}$s were: 7.12, 124.70, 4.06, 0.92, 0.14, and 0.16 for age (in years), correct responses, incorrect responses (i.e. miscues), failures, additions and omissions for grade- II children. Accompanying SDs were: 12.02, 3.01, 2.52, 0.97, 0.35, & 0.37. For grade-V children these $\overline{X}$s were: 10.10, 407.90, 12.68, 2.18, 0.48, and 1.76. Accompanying SDs were: 4.30, 8.33, 6.44, 1.91, 0.71, and 1.45.

Incorrect reading responses (miscues) produced by each *S* were then qualitatively analysed to assess the readers' reading strategy. These responses were analysed to see the extent of use of orthographic cues and context cues during reading. So far as the use of orthographic cues were concerned the miscues were analysed for target—miscue similarity for different letter positions i.e. for initial letter position, end letter position, middle-letter positions and also for number of letters similar irrespective of their positions. These values for different grade levels are given in Table 2.1. Similarity numbers were converted into proportions by dividing them by the corresponding numbers in the target words. This was done to make the similarity indicators comparable. These proportions are also presented in Table 2.1. Figures 2.1 and 2.2 present these proportions.

In order to see if these proportions were significantly different across two grades, *Z* tests for significance of difference between proportions were done. These *Z* values are also given in the bottom row of Table 2.1. None of these *Z* values, however, were significant.

Besides looking for orthographic cue use during reading, miscue analyses were done to look into use of semantic and syntactic cues during reading. Miscues were analysed for their semantic acceptability or unacceptability and also for their syntactic acceptability or unacceptability. Table 2.1 shows the total number of miscues that were semantically acceptable; semantically unacceptable, syntactically acceptable; and syntactically unacceptable. These figures were then converted into proportions by dividing them by the total number of miscues. This was done to make them comparable. These proportions are also given in Table 2.1. This table also gives the results of *Z* tests for significance of difference between these proportions across grades. The *Z* scores were significant for semantically acceptable, syntactically acceptable and syntactically unacceptable miscues; the proportions for first two being higher for grade-V *S*s. This implies that comparing grade-II and V *S*s; even when grade-V *S*s failed to read a word correctly they were more likely to give a meaningful and gramatically correct substitute for the target word.

Discussion and Conclusion

Miscue analysis is a widely used technique to infer about the reading strategy of a reader (Goodman, 1969; Burke, 1977; Potter, 1980, and

TABLE 2.1: Proportions for orthographic similarity, semantic and syntactic acceptability of miscues produced by grade-II and V children

Grade		Miscue-Target		Orthographic Similarity		Semantic Acceptability		Syntactic Acceptability	
		Initial letter	Total letters irrespective of position	End letter	Middle letters	Acceptable	Unacceptable	Acceptable	Unacceptable
II		107	342	106	103	64	135	63	136
		(203)	(607)	(203)	(189)				
	Proportions	.527	.563	.522	.544	.315	.670	.310	.660
V		414	1347	359	496	320	294	322	296
		(614)	(2140)	(614)	(879)				
	Proportions	.674	.629	.584	.564	.521	.478	.524	.482
	Z Values	1.50	0.67	0.62	0.54	2.10*	1.59	2.18*	1.91*

*p < .05

Note: Numbers in parentheses present the total number of letters that existed in the given position in the target words

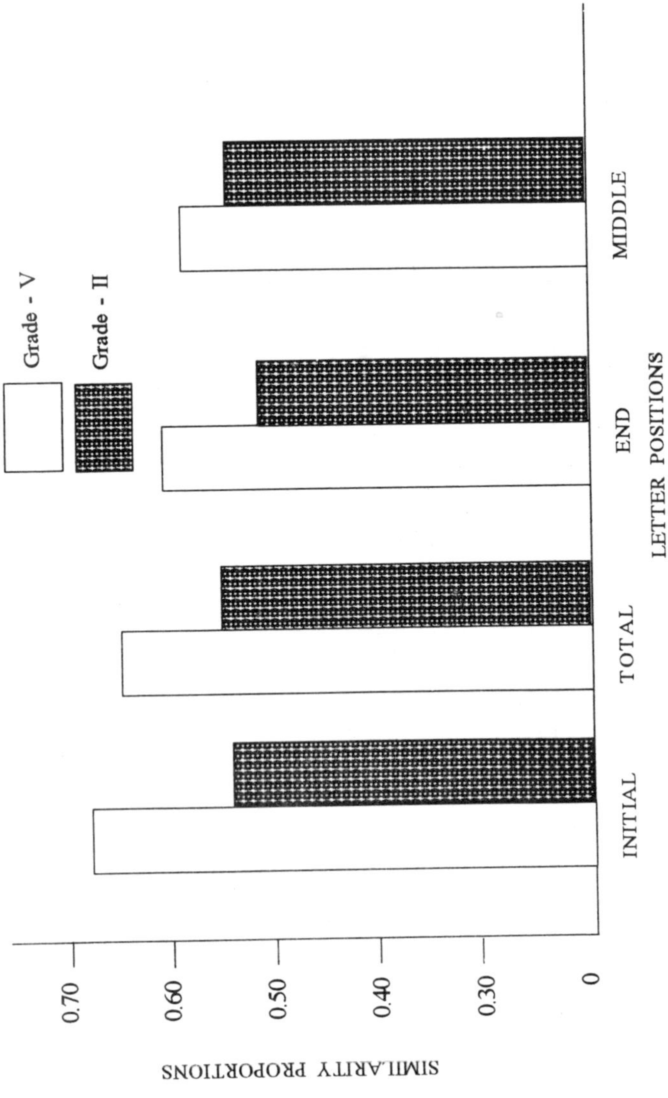

FIG. 2.1: Miscue-target-similarity proportions for various letter positions.

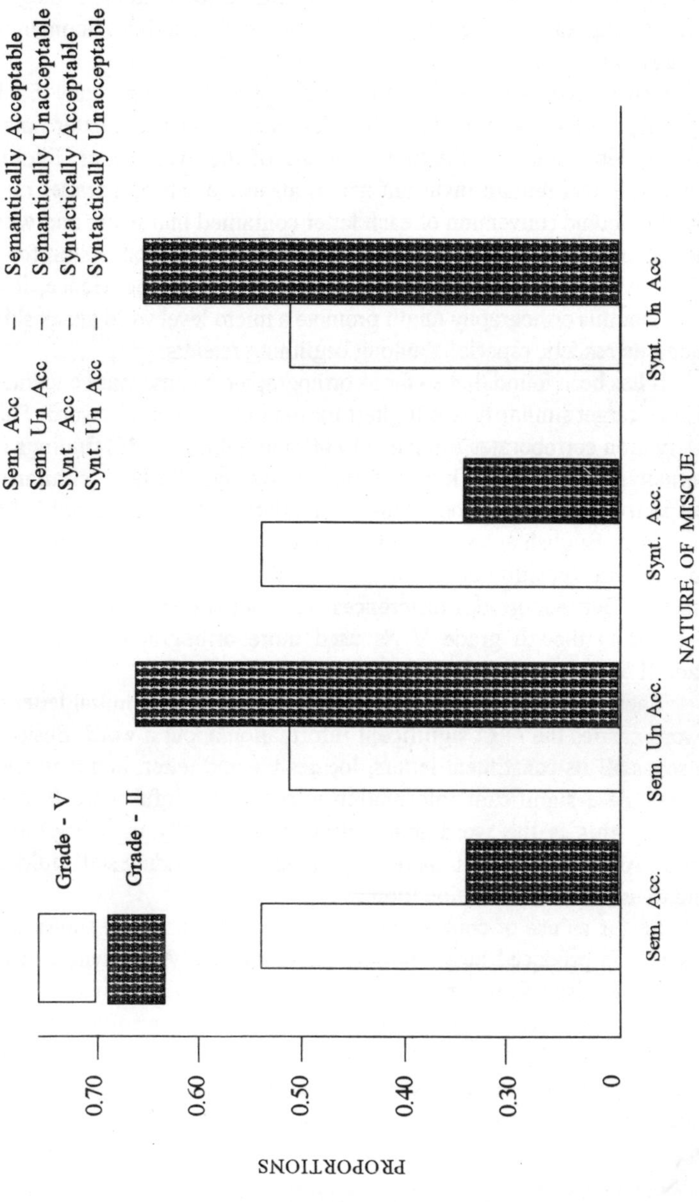

FIG. 2.2: The proportions of semantic and syntactic acceptibility of miscues.

reading strategy by revealing the causes of successful reading performance as well as the causes of unsuccessful reading performance. The present study used this procedure to locate the reading strategies of beginning readers reading in Oriya orthography; and developmental changes in it.

Oriya orthography is a syllabic type of phonetic orthography. Each letter is pronounceable by itself. Besides, each letter has a letter name and this letter name is the phonic sound of the given letter. Phonic sound of letters remain invariant across all usage. Thus, a reader may give the phonic conversion of each letter contained in a word, and with this apporach he can end up giving the correct sound conversion for a written word without scanning the whole word at a time. Hence, it is likely that this orthography might promote a micro level word attack skill among its readers, especially among beginning readers.

It has been found that so far as orthographic cue use was concerned miscue- target similarity was highest for the initial letter of a word. This observation corroborates Francis' (1984) and Sahu's (1985) findings in English orthography. This is followed by total letters' similarity irrespective of their positions. This substantiates Sahu's (1985 and 1987) findings in English as well as in Oriya orthography. This is followed by the end letter position confirming Francis' (1984) and Sahu's (1985) findings. Between-grades differences were not statistically significant (Table 2.1) though grade V *S*s used more orthographic cues than grade-II *S*s.

These findings mean that for beginning readers the initial letter of a word carries the most significant information about a word. Besides, he scans all its constituent letters, locates the end letter, and then tries to cast these significant information into a meaningful word format. Probably this is the word-attack strategy, especially of a beginning reader. And, probably with increasing mastery over reading skill children tend to use these information more.

So far as use of context cues is concerned, Table 2.1 shows that grade-V *S*s produced larger number of semantically and syntactically acceptable miscues and fewer number of semantically and syntactically unacceptable miscues than grade-II *S*s. Table 2.1 shows that three out of these four differences were statistically significant. These findings mean that with increasing mastery over reading skills, even when children read a word incorrectly, they tend to end up in giving meaningful and grammatical substitutes. Use of semantic and syntactic cues increases over age and grade.

The findings thus show that beginning reading makes use of orthographic, semantic and syntactic cues; and use of these cues increases with increasing age and grade levels. So far as use of orthographic and semantic-syntactic cues by beginning readers is concerned English and Oriya orthographies behave similaraly.

Summary

The present study aimed to look into the developmental changes in the oral reading strategies of primary grade children reading in Oriya orthography. The design was a 2 x 2 factorial design, with 2 sex groups (boys and girls) being orthogonally combined into 2 grade levels (grades-II and V). Fifty sample cases were randomly drawn from each grade level, thus the total N= 100. Grade-appropriate oral reading tasks were administered on all the *S*s. Miscues produced by *S*s were analysed to assess their reading strategies. Data analysis did not reveal any significant sex difference in oral reading strategies within a given grade level. So far as use of orthographic cues were concerned, it was observed that grade V *S*s used these cues to a greater extent than grade-II *S*s; but between-grades differences were not statistically significant. So far as use of semantic and syntactic cues were concerned, it was observed that grade-V children used these cues more than grade-II children, and this difference was statistically significant. Results have been interpreted in the light of acquisition and development of language skills in children.

SECTION- II

LEXICAL ACCESS

3

LEXICAL ACCESS IN ORIYA ORTHOGRAPHY

The Impact of Suppression Condition

So far as lexical access in reading is concerned two different models have been proposed. One group of researchers propose a direct print-to-lexicon approach in reading (Frith, 1979; Goodman & Goodman, 1979; Smith, 1979). On the other hand, some other researchers propose an indirect phonetically midiated approach for getting meaning from the prints. They propose that graphemes are first converted into phonetic bases before the reader gets meaning from the print (Liberman & Shankweiler, 1979; Perfetti & Lesgold, 1979; Zifack, 1981). The former model is known as the direct or the immediate lexical access model and the later is known as the indirect or mediated lexical access model. However, McCusker, Hillinger and Bias (1981) made an extensive review of research in the field and propose of a dual access model. It is proposed that subjects possess the capability of using both visual mediation and phonological recoding as routes from print to meaning and they have a fair amount of flexibility in determining when they are using one or the other. It is pointed out that high frequency words are probably accessed through a visual representation only, but low frequency words are accessed using a phonological recoding process. In the later case, phonological representation is used as an aid to comprehension which enable the activation of individual lexical entry to persist long enough till semantic integration is achieved. Phonological mediation is used with difficult, infrequent or unfamiliar materials and also in tasks that emphasise storage and processing in depth. This is used by subjects who have poor fluency in reading. Though McCusker *et al.* (1981) observations have not been accepted by all the researchers (Gullentag,

---

Co-author Sanjita Mishra

1982), yet it seems to be a plausible resolution of the controversy.

So far as writing systems are concerned, orthographies could be broadly devided into three categories such as : logographic, syllabic and alphabetic types (Hockett, 1970; Taylor, 1981; Varshney, 1988). Again on the basis of grapheme-to-phonic correspondence orthographies could be devided into phonetic or non-phonetic orthographies (Wagner & Torgesen, 1987). It is now an established fact that different orthographies produce different modes for access into semantic system (Besner, 1990). Besner views that reading of syllabic Japanese is more closely tied to articulatory activity than is the phonological code utilised while reading alphabetic English. Yamada, Imai and Ikebe (1990) looked into the lexical access route when subjects read Japanese syllabic *kana* script. Results supported a dual route hypothesis, and rejected the view that, *kana* words are accessed on the basis of phonological mediation alone . Such studies point to the possibility of different lexical access modes initiated by different orthographies. The present study looked into the possible lexical access route initiated by Oriya orthography, which is an alphabetic- syllabic type of phonetic orthography.

Besner (1990) looked into the phonological codes used by subjects for lexical access while reading English and Japanese scripts. He made subjects read real or pseudohonophones in Japanese or in English orthography under quiet reading condition; and under suppression condition aimed to disturb the articulatory process initiated by visual inputs. Under suppression condition subjects were asked to count 1 to 10 loudly while reading the items. Dependent measures observed were: lexical decision about the materials; and lexical decision making time for it. Results showed that suppression did not adversely affect the lexical decision time taken by subjects, when they read English. On the other hand suppression significantly affected the reading of Japanese *kana* which is a syllabic script. Response time here was significantly higher. Kimura (1984) also reports similar result. Thus whether suppression affects lexical decision and lexical decision-making time in the context of different orthographies is an unresolved question. The present study looked into the impact of the suppression condition on lexical decision and lexical decision making time, when subjects read Oriya orthography.

Method

Subjects

Fifty subjects from grade-V of a Government High School in

Bhubaneswar (capital city of Orissa, India) were taken as subjects for the present study. There were 25 girls and 25 boys in this group. Mean age of boys was 117.27 months with a standard deviation of 59.11; and mean age of girls was 113.89 months with a standard deviation of 47.39. It was decided to take subjects from grade-V, so that fluent oral reading is ensured, hence, possible impact of imperfect oral reading on subjects' lexical decision performance is avoided.

Oriya Language and Orthography

The Government of India officially recognises 18 different languages. They are: Assamese, Bengali, Gujrati, Hindi, Kashmiri, Konkani, Malayalam, Manipuri, Marathi, Nepali, Oriya, Punjabi, Sanskrit, Sindhi, Tamil, Telgu and Urdu. Hindi is used as the official language and English continues to be the subsidiary offical language.

These 18 different languages can, in fact, be grouped into four major linguistic families: Indo-Aryan, Dravidian, Austro-Asiatic and Tibeto-Chinese (Oomen, 1973). Languages belonging to a particular linguistic group bear a great deal of similarity to each other.

Assamese, Bengali, Gujrati, Hindi, and Oriya belong to the group of Indo-Aryan languages. They are basiclly different regional deviations of one basic language, i.e. Sanskrit. Though these five different languages have different scripts, they share a good deal of commonality among themselves. Pattanayak (1985) views Oriya as a member of eastern sub-branches of Indo-Aryan branch of Indo-European language family.

Oriya is the officially recognised language of the State of Orissa. It has two major local dialects: Sambalpuri Oriya and Cuttacki Oriya, spoken by western and eastern people of Orissa respectively. The tribal population of Orissa speak many tribal languages which includes Kondh, Kui, Kolha and many other languages. Inspite of these differences, children are taught to read and write in standard Oriya language, which is the media and book language. This standard language is used in text-books, news papers and magazines; and also in electronic media.

The Oriya orthography in use at present consists of 47 letters, out of these 12 are vowels and 35 are consonants. The typical way of writing Oriya consists of making two different circles, a smaller one; and a bigger one on the top of it. Distinguishing features are made in either or both of these circles and make-up a letter.

Apart from 47 letters in Oriya writing system vowels can be symbolically added to different consonants. When vowels are symbolically appended to a consonant, it is called a *matra.* Addition of a *matra* slightly changes the phonic sound of the consonant. These *matras* in combination with different consonants provide for a wide variety of spelling possibilities which in turn, provides a very wide scope for meaning differences of different words.

Besides, some consonants represented in the from of symbols could also be appended to other consonants. When a consonant symbol is used along with another consonant, it is called a *phala*. Addition of a *phala* to a consonant goes to make a compound consonant or a conjuct character. However, addition of a *matra* or a *phala* changes the phonetic representation of the concerned letter.

In addition, Oriya orthography provides for combinations of different consonants which are called *yuktakshyars* (Praharaj, 1936; Padhi, 1971). These *yuktakshyars* can be viewed as cluster graphemes.

Apart from *matras, phalas,* and *yuktakshyaras,* there are a few characters in Oriya orthography involving *doubling* of a single consonant. Such a character is written by putting the original consonant and by appending a symbolic representation of the same consonant to it. Such doubled characters retain the original phonic representation of the consonant but with a greater emphasis on it.

These *matras, phalas, yuktakshyars* and *doublings,* making conjuct consonants or cluster graphemes, make writing in Oriya orthography difficult and its reading complicated, though they contribute to the richness of the writing system and also to that of the language. Lingustic nuances and shades of expression in literature and other forms of creative writings make use of this facet of the writing system. Richness of Oriya literature owes a lot to these subtleties in its writing. However, each letter is pronounceable by itself, hence the orthography can be viewed to be syllabic in nature; and the phonetic mapping of each letter remains almost invariant, hence the orthography can also be viewed to be phonetic in nature. Thus, Oriya orthography can be viewed to be a syllabic type of phonetic orthography.

Comparison with English Orthography

English and Oriya writing systems are both alphabetic in nature and follow a left to right directionality in writing and reading.

In English writing system each letter stands for a phoneme. The writing system consists of five vowels and twenty-one consonants. But, unlike in Oriya writing system letters are not pronunceable by themselves. Though each letter has a name, the name is not the invariable phonic sound of the given letter. Combinations of letters make pronunceable units or syllables. Grapheme-to-phoneme correspondence is not invariant in English orthography. Each letter has a name but its phonemic representation depends upon the word context in which it appears. Unlike in Oriya writing system, English does not have a built-in phonetics nor is the grapheme-phoneme correspondence invariant.

Implications for Reading Strategy

So far as oral reading is concerned, English being an alphabetic, non-phonetic type of orthography would demand a wholistic view of the word before it is phonetically mapped. This is necessary since letters donot have invariant sound representations rather their pronounceations are dependent upon the word context in which they appear; and on the orthographic rules of the writing system. Thus, phonemic conversion of individual letters would not render a correct oral reading of the whole word.

On the other hand, Oriya orthography being a syllabic type of phonetic orthography, has almost invariant sound representations of letters. Thus, phonemic conversion of individual letters contained in a word may lead to a correct oral reading of the whole word. Hence, a wholistic view of the word may not be necessary for a correct reading. This, in turn, may produce a large number of word-callers.

Pilot Testing

The study aimed to include 40 real words of Oriya and 40 parallel pseudohomophones (pseudohomophones sound like real words, but are not spelled like real words) into account. In order to get a sample of 40 real words initially 50 words were randomly selected from the Oriya language textbook of grade- IV. All the children presently reading in grade-V had exposure to this text book during their previous year of schooling. A random sample of 10 children were selected for the pilot study and they were asked to read these 50 words. Then the experimenter dictated these words and these 10 *S*s were asked to write down these words. On the basis of the reading and writing responses these 50 words were assessed for their difficulty levels for reading and spelling. Words which elicited perfect reading and spelling were taken into account. A few words with 10 per cent difficulty levels in reading and/or spelling were also included. Thus, the sample of real words were ensured to produce almost correct reading and spelling from grade-V children.

A parallel list of 40 pseudohomophones were formulated. This was done by incorporating spelling errors into the words. But care was taken to ensure that the phonetic conversion of the pseudohomophones matches with that of the corresponding real word.

Design

The study was based on a 2 X 2 factorial design with two levels on the testing condition and two levels on the nature of the reading material. The levels on testing condition were: no-suppression and suppression conditions, and the levels on the nature of reading materials were: real words and pseudohomophones. The dependent measures observed were: lexicality decision about the words; and lexicality decision making time. Table 3.1 is the schematic presentation of the design of the study.

TABLE 3.1: Schematic presentation of the sesign of the study

		Nature of the Reading Material		
		Real words	Pseudohomophones	Total
Testing conditions	No-suppression	N=20	N=20	N=40
	Suppression	N=20	N=20	N=40
	Total	N=40	N=40	N=80

The subjects had to read aloud the real words and the pseudohomophones under no-suppression and suppression testing conditions. And, they had to report if such words exist in Oriya lexicon. Lexicality decisions and decision making time was being recorded for each item. Each reading item was individually presented on a card, and subjects were tested individually.

So far as testing conditions are concerned under no-suppression condition the subjects had to read the words in quiet situation and had to give their decision. On the other hand, under suppression condition, similar presentation of real and pseudohomophones were done, but during the presentation subjects were asked to count the numbers 1 to 10 loudly. This procedure was supposed to disturb the articulatory activity which may follow visual input from print (Besner, 1990).

Results

A *'t'* test for significance difference in mean ages of boys and girls, preceded by an *'F'* test for homogeneity of variance, showed that the variances were homogeneous ($F = 1.25$; $df = 24/24$; $p > .05$); and the mean difference was insignificant ($'t' = 22$; $df = 48$; $p > .05$). Significance of difference between boys' and girls' means for lexicality decisions and lexicality decision-making times for real words and pseudohomophones under no-suppression and suppression conditions were tested. These differences were insignificant in almost all the cases. Hence, data across sex groups were pooled together. These means for no suppression condition were: 42.10 secs and 47.62 secs. for real words and pseudohomophones respectively. The accompanying standard deviations were: 5.21, and 11.08. The mean values for suppression condition were: 28.00 secs. and 29.78 secs. for real words and pseudohomophones with accompanying standard deviation values of 2.46, and 3.36. Here, it can be seen that no-suppression condition produced unusually longer time, and pseudohomophones produced longer time. Table 3.2 presents the total number of real words and pseudohomophones judged to be positive for lexicality under no-suppression and suppression conditions.

TABLE 3.2: Total number of real words and pseudohomophones judged positive for lexicality decision

		Nature of Reading Material	
		Real words	Pseudohomophones
Testing Condition	No-suppresssion	990	984
	Suppression	982	982

Note: Total number of possible responses in each case was 1000.

A chi-square test for the total number of real words and pseudohomophones judged positive for lexicality yielded a chi-square value of 0.961. With $df = 1$, this value was insignificant. This means that lexicality decision was unaffected by the nature of the reading material; also by testing condition.

To see if reading materials and/or testing conditions produced any significant variance a 2x2 ANOVA was done. This is reported in Table 3.3.

Discussion and Conclusion

The present study aimed to look into the mode of lexical access in Oriya orthography when articulatory activity is suppressed. Oriya is an

TABLE 3.3: Summary of 2 (real words and pseudohomophones) X 2 (no-suppression and suppression conditions) analysis of variance for lexicality decision time with repeated observations on both the factors

Sources of variance	Sum of squares	Degrees of Freedom	Mean square variance	*F* ratio	*p* level
Between (*S*s)	6997.62	49	—	—	—
Within (*S*s)	18828.25	150	—	—	—
A (Testing Condition)	12752.04	1	12752.04	293.12**	$p < .01$
A X *S*s (Error I)	2131.71	49	43.50	—	—
B (Nature of Reading materials)	666.12	1	666.12	44.73**	$p < .01$
B X *S*s (Error II)	129.62	49	14.89	—	—
AB	174.85	1	174.85	3.61	$p > .01$
A X B X *S*s (Error III)	2373.90	49	48.45	—	—
Total	25825.87	199	—	—	—

** $p < .01$

alphabetic-syllabic type of phonetic orthography; and the study took high frequency real words and parallel pseudohomophones into account. After the presentation of each letter string *S*s were asked to say if such words exist in Oriya lexicon disregarding the spelling errors, whenever they existed. Under suppression testing condition overt phonetic articulation was being intervened by asking *S*s to count numbers 1 to 10.

Results show that lexical decision was positive for almost all the real words and pseudohomophones. Suppression of overt articulation did not affect lexical decision adversely (Table 3.2). This probably means that the phonetic Oriya orthography produces phonological code before being mapped into semantic space. But in case the word is a familiar word with high frequency of use, the phonetic code leading to lexical access is so automatic that it does not need an overt articulation in order that semantic access is available. However, such an overt articulation of the phonetic code may be necessary in case of unfamiliar or less frequently used words or words with difficult spelling patterns.

Moreover, so far as lexical decision time is concerned, the present study shows that pseudohomophones need more time for lexical access than real words, and no-suppression condition produced higher decision making time than suppression condition (Table 3.3).

The observation that pseudohomophones needed more time than real words for lexical access could be due to the fact that phonological codes initiated by real words and pseudohomophones remaining the same, given graphemic input and visual orthographic image of the word will match in case of the former, and will not match in case of the later. This mismatch will create confusion and pose a problem before lexical decision is made for them (i.e. for pseudohomophones). Since *S*s were instructed to make decisions without taking into account the correctness of spelling, the phonetic code initiated probably has prevailed and guided *S*s through lexical decision. Nevertheless, the graphemic input and visual orthographic image (of the word) mismatch delayed the decision making time.

Other observation pertaining to decision-making time was that, this time was higher under no-suppression condition than under suppression condition. This finding is perplexing. Observations till date have obtained either equal (for English, an alphabetic orthography) or lesser time (for Japanese *kana,* a syllabic script) for no-suppression condition, when compared with that of the suppression condition (Besner, 1990). That is, suppression of overt articulation either does not retard or retards lexical decision time; but has never been observed to accelerate it, as it has happened in the present experiment.

A possible explanation for this could be *S*s' extra alertness under suppression condition to give the decision. Phonetic mapping and mediation being almost automatic for fluent oral readers for very familiar words in the phonetic Oriya orthography *S*s took usual time to respond under no-suppression condition; but because of extra alertness and/or anxiety created by suppression condition, tried to give their responses at the earliest under this set up. This might have resulted in lowered reaction time under suppression condition. However, further research is needed to settle this question.

Thus, the present study shows that for very familiar words, and that too for fluent oral readers, Oriya orthography probably elicits phonetic codes which are highly automatic, and hence, do not need overt articulation. And, interference with overt articulation under such circumstances decreases decision-making time.

Summary

So far as lexical access in reading is concerned immediate and mediated lexical access models have been proposed. Researchers propose that different orthographies might be initiating different lexical access routes. The present study looked into the possible lexical access route initiated by the alphabatic-syllabic and phonetic Oriya orthography.

Lexicality decisions and decision making times for real and parallel pseudohomophones were assessed under no-suppression and suppression testing conditions. The sample (N = 50) was drawn from grade - V, ensuring a fluent oral reading. On the basis of a pilot study 40 real words, for which *S*s (subjects) showed almost perfect reading and spelling abilities, were taken into account. A parallel list of 40 pseudohomophones were constructed with minor spelling deviations. These 40 words and 40 pseudohomophones were randomly assigned over no-suppression and suppression testing conditions with 20 reading materials per condition. All the 50 *S*s took all the four testing situations. Variables observed were : lexicality decision; and lexicality decision-making time.

Results revealed no sex difference over dependent measures. Lexicality decisions were positive for almost all the reading materials. So far as lexicality decision time was concerned, it was found to be affected by testing condition (i.e. no-suppression *vs.* suppression testing conditions): and nature of the reading material (i.e. real *vs.* pseudohomophones). Decision-making time was higher under no-suppression condition, and for pseudohomophones. Results have been interpreted with reference to the nature of Oriya orthography; reading competence of the reader; and nature of the reading materials. It was concluded that probably under existing circumstances overt articulation of phonetic code was not necessary for lexical access.

4

LEXICAL ACCESS IN ORIYA ORTHOGRAPHY
Observations in Unfamiliar Word Context

Lexical access mode is probably orthography-dependent (Besner, 1990; Yamada, Imai, Ikebe, 1990; Yamada, Mitarai and Yoshida, 1991; Sahu and Mishra, 1993). Observations in English orthography show that reading in this orthography is not very much dependent on articulation of phonological code. But observations in Japanese orthography show that reading in this orthography is very much dependent upon articulation of phonological code initiated by the graphemic input. Suppression of this articulation impedes reading. English is an alphabetic (and non-phonetic) orthography; and Japanese is a syllabic orthography. Observation in Oriya orthography, which is a syllabic (and at the same time a phonetic) orthography show that with very familiar words, reading is not very much phonetic code dependent. It may be pointed out here that apart from division of orthographies into logographic, syllabic and alphabetic types they can be grouped into phonetic and non-phonetic orthographies (Wagner and Torgesen, 1989). Broadly, a phonetic orthography is one, where grapheme-to-phoneme correspondence is almost invariant; graphemes retain their phonetic mappings across their uses in different word contexts. On the other hand, a non-phonetic orthography is one, where, grapheme-to-phoneme correspondence varies depending upon the word context in which the grapheme appears. Besides, Sgall (1987) also differentiates between phonemic and non-phonemic orthographies. A phonemic orthography is one, where a grapheme stands for a phoneme; a phoneme being a part of a speech sound. English orthography, apart from being alphabetic and non-phonetic could be viewed to be phonemic, where, each alphabet stands for a

---

Co-author Sanjita Mishra

phoneme. It may be pointed out here that reading in the context of a phonemic orthography would necessarily demand orthography-specific sound blending skills from the reader, but reading in the context of a syllabic orthography may not demand sound blending skills from a reader.

Lexical access modes apart from being orthography dependent, may also depend upon the familiarity of the word (Mc Cusker, Hillinger and Bias, 1981). The present study aimed to look into the lexical access mode for less familiar Oriya words. For this purpose it was proposed to use Besner's (1990) phonetic articulation suppression technique.

Method

Subjects

Fifty subjects from grade-V of a Government High School of Bhubaneswar, Orissa, were taken as the subjects (*S*s) for this study. There were 25 girls and 25 boys in this group. Mean ($\bar{X}$) age of boys was 117.89 months with a SD of 6.27; and $\bar{X}$ age of girls was 117.57 months with a SD of 2.64. Boys and girls did not differ significantly on their mean age ($t = 0.23$; $p > .05$). Subjects were selected from grade V, so as to ensure fluent oral reading of Oriya words.

Description about Oriya language and orthography, its comparison with English orthography, and implications for reading strategy are given in Sahu and Mishra (1993).

Pilot Testing

This study being second in series of the study aiming to assess lexical access modes used in Oriya orthography, took 40 unfamiliar words along with 40 parallel pseudohomophones into account. Pseudohomophones sound like real words but have spelling errors in them. In order to get 40 unfamiliar words initially 100 words from language text books of grades-V and VI were selected. A piolot sample of 10 children from grade-V were asked to read these 100 words. On the basis of percentage of success at reading, words were finally selected for use in the present experiment. Forty words with 90 per cent to 100 per cent difficulty level (i.e. percentage of success at reading being 10 per cent or 0 per cent respectively) were finally selected for the study. This procedure ensured that these words were unfamiliar for grade-V children.

A parallel list of 40 pseudohomophones were formulated for these 40 real words. This was done by incorporating spelling errors into real words. Care was taken to see that the phonetic conversion of the pseudohomophones matched with that of the corresponding real word.

Design

This study was based on 2 X 2 factorial design with two levels on testing conditions and two levels on nature of reading materials. The levels on testing condition were no-suppression and suppression conditions, and the levels on the nature of reading materials were real words and pseudohomophones. The dependent measures observed were lexicality decision about the words; and lexicality decision-making time.

The subject had to read aloud the real words and the pseudohomophones under no suppression and suppression testing conditions and, had to report if such words exist in Oriya lexion. Lexicality decision and decision-making time was being recorded for each reading item. Each reading item was individually presented on a card, and subjects were individually tested.

So far as testing conditions are concerned under no suppression condition the subjects had to read the words in quiet situation and had to give their decision. On the other hand, under suppression condition, similar presentation of real words and pseudohomophones were done, but during the presentation subjects were asked to count numbers 1 to 10 loudly. This procedure was supposed to disturb the articulatory activity which may follow visual input from print (Besner, 1990).

Results

Tables 4.1 and 4.2 present means ($\overline{X}$s) and standard deviations (SDs) for lexicality decisions and decision making times for real words and pseudohomophones under no suppression and suppression conditions respectively.

Significance of difference between boys' and girls' $\overline{X}$s were tested. These differences were significant for lexical decision time under suppression condition for real and pseudohomophones. All other mean differences were insignificant.

Since the sex group differences existed on some significant dependent measures data accross sex group were not pooled together, and further analyses were done for boys and girls separately.

Table 4.3 presents the total number of real words and pseudohomophones judged to be positive under no suppression and suppression conditions.

A Chi-square (χ^2) test for above lexical decisions was made. The chi-square value was 10.79 with a $df = 1$ and $p < .01$. This implies that lexical decisions were adversely affected by suppression condition; and pseudohomophones.

TABLE 4.1 Means ($\overline{X}$s) and standard deviations (SDs) for lexicality decisions and lexicality decision-making time for real words and pseudohomophones under no-suppression condition

		Real Words		Pseudohomophones	
		Lexicality decision (positive)	Lexicality decision Time (in secs)	Lexicality decision (positive)	Lexicality decision Time (in secs)
	$\overline{X}$	17.76	57.72	16.44	64.92
Boys	SD	1.34	11.09	1.29	13.07
	$\overline{X}$	18.40	53.16	17.08	58.36
Girls	SD	1.26	14.02	1.57	14.40
'*t*' ratio		1.74	1.28	0.51	1.69

Note: None of the '*t*' ratios was significant.

TABLE 4.2: Means and standard deviations (SDs) for lexicality decisions and lexicality decision-making time for real words and pseudohomophones under suppression condition

		Real Words		Pseudohomophones	
		Lexicality decision (positive)	Lexicality decision Time (in secs)	Lexicality decision (positive)	Lexicality decision Time (in secs)
	$\overline{X}$	17.16	108.92	15.48	136.48
Boys	SD	1.59	28.02	1.81	28.42
	$\overline{X}$	17.28	131.76	15.48	151.48
Girls	SD	1.71	21.83	1.72	24.13
'*t*' ratios		0.25	3.21**	0.50	2.01*

**$p < .01$

* $p < .05$

TABLE 4.3: Total number of real words and pseudohomophones judged positive for lexicality decision

		Nature of Reading Material	
		Real words	Pseudohomophones
Testing condition	No-suppression	904	838
	Suppression	861	772

Table 4.4 presents summary tables for 2 X 2 (i.e. 2 testing conditions X 2 types of reading materials) analyses of variance with repeated observation on both the factors, for boys and girls.

TABLE 4.4: Summaries of 2x2 analyses of varience for lexicality decision time with repeated observations on both factors

Sources of Variance	*df*	Boys		Girls	
		MSV	*F*	MSV	*F*
Testing Condition	1	94187.61	220.91**	184298.49	371.12**
Nature of Reading Material	1	7551.61	67.84**	3881.29	49.97**
Interaction	1	2590.81	2.01	1317.71	63.94**

$^{**}p < .01$

Table 4.4 shows that boys sample yielded significant *F* ratios for testing condition variance and also for nature of reading materials variance. It means that for boys lexicality decision time was higher for suppression condition than it was for no suppression condition; and the lexicality decision time for pseudohomophones was higher than for real words.

Table 4.4 shows that girls' sample yielded significant *F* ratios for testing condition variance, nature of reading materials variance, and their interaction. It means, that for this group of subject's lexical decision time was higher under suppression condition than it was for no suppression condition; lexical decision time for pseudohomophones was higher than it was for real words. Besides, a significant interaction means that suppression of articulation increases the lexical decision time for both real and pseudohomophones, but this increment was disproportionately high for pseudohomophones. Figure 4.1 depicts this interaction effect.

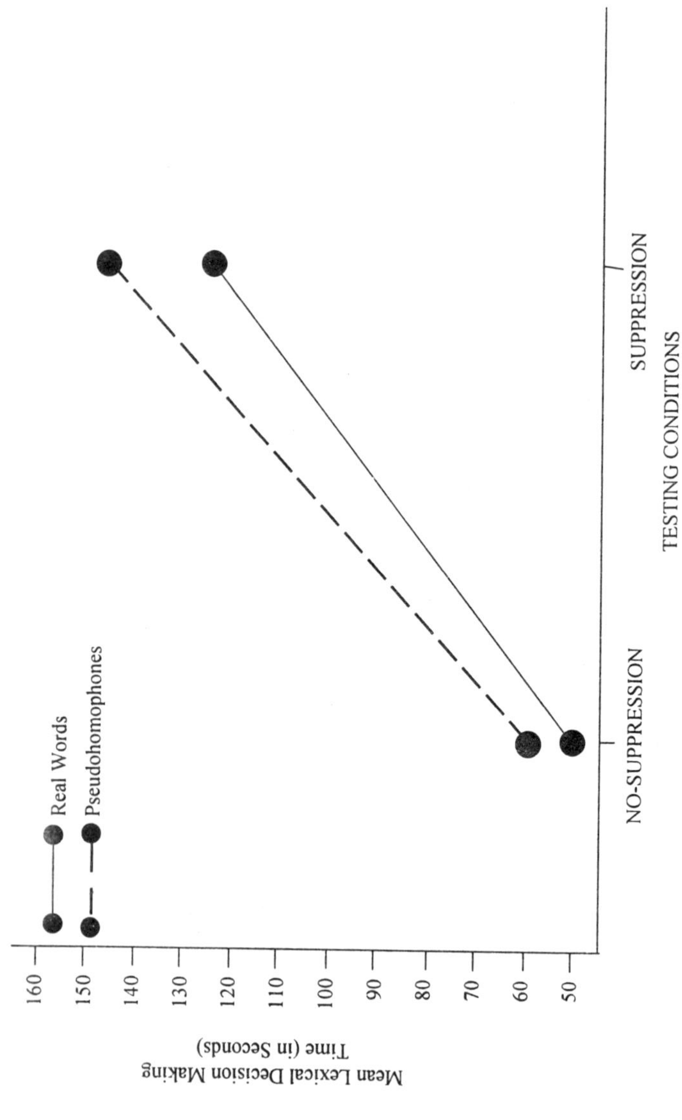

FIG. 4.1: Figure showing mean lexical decision-making time taken by girls for real words and pseudohomophones under no-suppression and suppression conditions

Discussion and Conclusion

This study looked into lexical access mode in Oriya orthography using unfamiliar words. Chi-square result shows that suppression of articulation adversely affects lexical decision; and lexicality decision time was higher for pseudohomophones than it was for real words. These observations are different from the observations made by Sahu and Mishra (1993). The previous study used very familiar words. They were probably as good as "sight words" for the subjects hence, did not demand conscious effort from subjects for their correct reading who were fluent oral readers. On the other hand, the present study used words which were unfamiliar for the subjects. These words probably would demand conscious effort from the subject to be read correctly. Hence suppression of phonetic code articulation would disturb the process of reading, and the process of lexicality decision. Probably this is the reason why suppression adversely affected lexicality decision in the present study.

So far as the nature of reading materials are concerned pseudohomophones have produced lesser number of positive lexical decisions than real words. In the present study real words themselves were unfamiliar for subjects. When spelling errors were added to this dimension of unfamiliarity, it probably resulted in a decreased number of positive lexical decision.

Table 4.4 shows that both boys and girls yielded significant *F* ratios for testing condition and nature of reading materials variances. In case of both the subject groups suppression of articulation led to increase in lexical decision time. Oriya orthography is a syllabic and phonetic orthography. Each letter is pronounciable by itself and the built-in phonetic remains in-variant across all uses of letter. Correct reading of unfamiliar words in such a writing system would take the help of phonetic code initiated by visual graphemic input. Interference or suppression of this code would interfere with the very process of reading. This inturn, would demand greater cognitive effort from subject leading to increased reading time. This observation is significant and establishes the fact that the reading of unfamiliar words in Oriya takes the help of phonetic code mediation. That is, under such circumstances, it is the mediated lexical access model which holds good. Sahu and Mishra (1993) and this study go together to establish the McCuskar, Hillinger and Bias's (1981) contention that both immediate and mediated lexical access modes are available to fluent readers and the reader uses any one of these modes or a combination of both modes for reading. Under familiar and easy text reading conditions immediate mode is used and under unfamiliar and difficult text reading conditions mediated mode is used.

Both boys and girls have yielded significant *F* ratios for nature of reading material variance. Pseudohomophones increased the lexicality decision-making time. Real words in the present study were unfamiliar for subjects. Some of the lexical decisions even for real words were negative. It means that reading and making lexical decisions of real words were quite difficult for the present group of subjects. When spelling errors are added to this, as in case of pseudohomophones, the cognitive load increases and leads to higher reading time.

Table 4.4 shows that girls in present study yielded significant *F* ratio for the interaction variance. Lexical decision time increased for suppression conditions and also for pseudohomophones. But this increment was disproportionately high for pseudohomophones under suppression condition. This is probably due to the fact that this condition puts maximum cognitive load on *S*s, hence reading and lexical decision time was highest.

Thus the present study shows that for reading unfamiliar Oriya words suppression of phonetic articulation adversely affects performance. This implies that for reading of such words phonetic mediation is helpful. The present study thus implicates at the fact that lexical access route in case of syllabic and phonetic Oriya orthography is probably mediated through phonetic code, especially in case of unfamiliar reading materials.

Summary

Lexical access modes could be orthography—dependent to some extent, i.e. though both mediated and immediate modes are available to a fluent reader, different orthographies might be weighing differently on one or the other mode for an access to lexicon. The present study looked into the possible lexical access mode of fluent oral readers reading unfamiliar words in Oriya orthography. Twenty five boys and twenty-five girls of grade-V were made to read real words and parallel pseudohomophones and make lexical decision under conditions of suppression of phonetic articulation; and no suppression of phonetic articulation. Dependent measures observed were lexical decision and lexical decision-making time. Results showed that lexicality decision was adversely affected by suppression condition; and also by pseudohomophone materials. So far as lexical decision time was concerned both groups of subjects took longer time under conditions of suppression and for pseudohomophones.

Girls here showed a significant interaction between the two variables indicating that lexical decision time taken under suppression conditions for pseudohomophones was the highest. Results have been interpreted in the light of the features of Oriya orthography vis-a-vis the impact of suppression on its reading. It has been concluded that reading unfamiliar text in Oriya orthography takes the help of articulation of phonetic code.

SECTION - III

COGNITIVE CORRELATES / DETERMINERS

5

INFORMATION PROCESSING, PLANNING, AND READING IN ORIYA ORTHOGRAPHY

Recent approaches in the field of cognition and education do not put emphasis on intelligence as a determiner, nor as an end product as such. Rather emphasis is laid on underlying cognitive processes, and strategies taken by a subject to arrive at a given response. Das, Kirby and Jarman (1979) propose of simultaneous and successive cognitive processes as underlying variables behind various educational outcomes. Besides, their model also propose of planning as a cognitive strategy in explaining various educational outcomes (Das, Naglieri and Kirby, 1994). Taking a link from Luria's (1970) concept of functional organisation of brain Das and his associates proposed of the concept of information processing and planning as an alternative model for cognitive abilities.

The model proposes that simultaneous and successive modes of processing the incoming information are available to the subject. Simultaneous processing refers to the act of processing the whole stimulus complex surveying all the bits at a time. On the other hand, successive information processing refers to processing of information in a serial order, taking one bit of the stimulus complex at a time and then proceeding to the next. After stimuli from the external world are fed into the central processing unit, planning and decision making processes come into play. It has been proposed that modes of information processing and planning taken together influence the cognitive performance.

Das and his associates have developed different measures for assessing simultaneous and successive processing abilities of subjects. Measures of simultaneous processing include Raven's Coloured Progressive Matrices (Raven, 1956), figure copying (Ilg and Ames,

---

Co-author Sujata Mohanty

1964) and memory for designs (Graham and Kendall, 1960). Digit span, visual short term memory, and free or serial recall have been used as successive processing measures.

Planning has been defined as a set of decisions or strategies an individual adopts and modifies to solve a problem and to reach a goal (Das, 1980). It refers to a process involved in non-routine selection of programmes for action, labelled as supervisory attentional system (Shallice, 1982). Luria (1966) however, defined planning as consisting of programming, regulation, and verification of behaviour. These definitions indicate at the directive and evaluative role of planning. Planning is not a routine behaviour. It is characterised by purpose under a given problem situation. It is self-generated and occurs in advance of action. It regulates behaviour, probably by using inner speech (Das, Naglieri, and Kirby, 1994). Measures of planning include trail making (Ashman, 1978), visual search, planned connections, planned composition and matching numbers (Das, Neglieri and Kirby, 1994).

Das's model of intellect have been applied to explain various cognitive functions. It has been applied to explain school achievement, learning disabilities, mental retardation, and language functions. So far as reading processes are concerned this model has been tried to explain reading achievement and reading disability in children. Broadly speaking it has been observed that both simultaneous and successive processes contribute to the reading competence of subjects (Das, Kirby and Jarman, 1979). Planning processes have also been found to contribute to reading and related processes (Ramey, 1985).

However, all these studies have been done in the context of English orthography. English is an alphabetic type of non-phonetic orthography. Researches across orthographies are needed to look into the generalisability of the above finding.

The present problem aimed to look into the imformation processing straegies and planning abilities of children reading in Oriya orthography. This study looked into the oral reading processes at two developmental points of reading skill acquisition. Oriya, is a syllabic type of phonetic orthography. Detailed descriptions about the features of Oriya orthography, its comparision with English orthography, and implications for reading strategies have been given in Sahu, Mohanty and Singh (1995).

Method

Design

The study was based on a 2 X 2 factorial model involving two grade levels (i.e., grades-II and V) and two sex groups (i.e., boys and girls). Sample size in each of the resulting four cells was 25. Thus the total N was 100.

Sample

Sample cases were randomly drawn from grades-II and V from a Government High School of Bhubaneswar, Orissa.

Tests and Tasks used

Measures of simultaneous processing, successive processing, planning and grade—appropriate oral reading tasks were administered on all the subjects.

Measures of Simultaneous Processing

Three such measures were used in the present study. They included block design test, test of similarities, and figures copying test (Ilg and Ames, 1964). Block design and similarities tests were taken from Bhatt's (1973) Gujarati Adaptation of Wechsler Intelligence Scale for Children.

Measures of Successive Processing

Here also three tests were taken. Digit span test (Bhatt, 1973), visual sequential memory test (Kirk, McCarthy and Krik, 1968) and serial recall test (Das *et al.,* 1979) were used as successive processing measures.

Measures of Planning Ability

Trail making (Ashman, 1978) test was used as the measure of planning in the present study. This test consists of three trials, starting with very easy and gradually increasing in difficulty. Each trial consists of connecting digits and/or letters as per a given sequence. Number of errors and time taken to complete each trial was recorded. Trail making test alongwith visual search test has been found to load on planning factor (Das, 1980).

Oral Reading Tasks

Grade-appropriate oral reading tasks were administered on all the subjects. These tasks were developed by Sahu and Pattnaik (1987) and have been shown to be reliable and valid. Oral reading tasks consist of a number of sentences to be read aloud by subject. These sentences are arranged in increasing difficulty level. As the subject reads sentences his exact responses are recorded, which are scored for number of words read correctly, number of words read incorrectly, number of additions, number of ommisions, and number of complete failures to read. Besides, time taken by subject to complete the task is also recorded.

All the above tests and tasks were individually administered on all subjects.

Results

Means ($\overline{X}$s) and standard deviation (SDs) for all the test scores were obtained. Significance of mean differences between boys and girls were tested applying *'t'* tests. In almost all the cases the *'t'* ratios were insignificant. This means that sex differences across the observed measures did not exist within a given grade level. Hence, data across sex groups were pooled together during further analyses. These $\overline{X}$s for grade-II were: 5.42 for block design (BD), 6.18 for figure copying (FC), 7.94 for similarities (Sim), 4.66 for digit span forward (DSF), 2.58 for digit span backward (DSB), 7.24 for digit span total (DST), 11.22 for visual sequential memory (VSM), and 62.72 for serial recall (SR) scores. Accompanying SDs were: 4.58, 2.19, 3.77, 0.80, 0.86, 1.24, 3.22 and 9.58. For this group the $\overline{X}$ planning and oral reading scores were: 38.04 (secs.) for trail making time trial 1, 57.10 for trial 2, 182.48 for trial 3, and 277.54 for total time. Accompanying SD values were: 30.56, 45.01, 104.75, and 138.28. Mean correct oral reading score was 101.66 with a SD of 43.64. For grade-V the mean values were: 18.00 (BD), 13.76 (FC), 21.12 (Sim), 5.46 (DSF), 3.94 (DSB), 9.40 (DST), 25.22 (VSM) and 63.06 (SR). Planning times (in secs.) were: 23.20, 30.72, 101.14 and 154.86. Correct oral reading $\overline{X}$ was 418.14. All these $\overline{X}$s had the following SD values, i.e. 14.59, 10.11, 5.37, 0.89, 0.65, 1.23, 5.09, 8.25, 7.24, 12.49, 46.28, 54.13, and 23.35.

In order to see how all the independent measures contributed to oral reading performance and to locate significant contributors, multiple correlations (Rs) followed by stepwise (forward) regression analyses were done. It was observed that at grades-II and V level some subjects scored very low on oral reading performance. These subjects also showed unsteady performance over other measures. Hence, it was decided to exclude scores beyond the range of $\overline{X} \pm 1$ SD on correct oral reading performance during computation of R and stepwise regression analyses. An inspection of raw scores showed that with this decision only poor performers were excluded. No *S* had oral reading score one standard deviation above the mean. At grade-II level there existed 8 such cases and at grade-V level there existed 6 such cases. Thus during multiple correlation and stepwise regression analyses N= 42 at grade-II level and N= 44 at grade-V level. It may be pointed out here that inclusion of outliers in analyses produces noise leading to erratic results.

Tables 5.1 and 5.2 present the results of R and forward stepwise regression.

Table 5.1 shows that at grade-II level all the 12 variables taken together yielded an R value of .52487 ($p < .01$) with correct oral reading score, contributing 27.54 per cent of variance to the dependent measure. Time taken at the second trial of the trail making test contributed significant variance to the correct reading performance. Apart from this variable no other measure contributed additional significant variance to the correct reading scores. Table 5.2 shows that at grade-V level the R between all the measures and the correct oral reading score was .42906 ($p = .02$) contributing 18.41 per cent of variance in the dependent measure. Here, time taken at the third trial of the trail making test and total time taken over all the three trials of the same test have been found to be significant contributors. It may be pointed out here that at grade II and grade V levels measures of planning have been found to contribute significant variances to correct oral reading performance. This finding is significant.

At this point it was decided to look into the intercorrelations between the predictor variables. Tables 5.3 and 5.4 present these intercorrelations for grades-II and V. Outliers were not included while running scores for intercorrelations.

So far as intercorrelations within simultaneous, successive and planning measures are concerned Table 5.3 shows that measures of simultaneous processing did not project strong intercorrelations. This is also true about the measures of successive processing excepting for digit span subscores. But, planning scores projected strong inter-correlations. It is only this factor that presented a strong cluster. Digit span scores did not correlate with any of the planning scores. Table 5.4

TABLE 5.1: Summary of multiple correlation and stepwise regression analysis for grade - II *Ss*.

Independent variables	Dependent variables	R	%ge of variance accounted for	Adjusted R^2	*F*	*p*	Significant predictor	Beta values & constant
BD, FC, Sim, DSF, DSB, DST, VSM, SR, Time 1, Time 2, Time 3, Tot Time	Correct Oral Reading Scores	.52487	27.5491	.25737	15.20953	$< .01$	Time 2 128.868364	-.163967 &

Note: Tot Time is total trail making time.

TABLE 5.2: Summary of multiple correlation and stepwise regression analyses for grade-V *Ss*

Independent variables	Variable droped	Dependent variables	R	%ge of variance accounted for	Adjusted R^2	*F*	*p*	Significant predictor (s)	Beta values & constant
BD, FC, Sim., DSF, DSB, DST, VSM, SR, Time 1, Time 2, Time 3, Tot Time	—	Correct Oral Reading Score	.42906	18.409	.14429	4.62529	$= .02$	Time 3 Tot Time	-.192455. .129513 & 424.910792
BD, FC, Sim, DSF, DSB, DST, VSM, SR, Time 1, Time 2, Time 3, Tot Time	Tot time	Correct Oral Reading Score	.30634	9.384	.07227	4.34962	$= .04$	Time 3	-.047135 & 430.326556

TABLE 5.3 : Inter-correlations between predictor variables for Grade-II (N = 42)

	BD	FC	Sim.	DSF	DSB	DST	VSM	SR	Time 1	Time 2	Time 3	Total Time
BD	—											
FC	.3968*	—										
Sim	-.2310	-.0160	—									
DSF	.0662	.1523	.2579	—								
DSB	.4553**	.1602	.3831*	.1149	—							
DST	.2733	.2094	.4321**	.7244**	.7680**	—						
VSM	.1309	.2070	.2188	.1261	.4215*	.3738*	—					
SR	-.0414	.0073	.2394	.4516**	.0474	.3240	.0155	—				
Time 1	-.2518	-.2131	-.2412	-.0245	-.1890	-.1470	-.0484	.1275	—			
Time 2	-.2537	-.2131	-.0997	.1646	-.2321	-.0550	-.1515	.2458	.5996**	—		
Time 3	-.0530	-.0117	-.1683	.0943	-.0347	.0367	-.1963	.1257	.1667	.2651	—	
Total Time	-.1781	-.1255	-.2138	.1193	-.1432	-.0225	-.2089	.2029	.5424**	.6590**	.8797**	—

** $p < .01$, * $p < .05$

TABLE 5.4 : Inter-correlations between the predictor variables, Grade - V (N=44)

	BD	FC	Sim.	DSF	DSB	DST	VSM	SR	Time 1	Time 2	Time 3	Total Time
BD	—											
FC	.0681	—										
Sim.	.2823	.0221	—									
DSF	.1432	.1182	.2885	—								
DSB	.3832*	.0138	.3411	.1495	—							
DST	.3215	.0964	.4049*	.8337**	.6706**	—						
VSM	.1828	-.3164	.1011	.1661	.1692	.2191	—					
SR	.2856	-.1708	-.0448	.0334	.0712	.0649	.2328	—				
Time 1	-.3831*	-.1567	-.1459	-.1156	-.0434	-.1110	.1404	.0389	—			
Time 2	-.3974*	-.0251	-.1606	.0261	-.2192	-.1029	-.0782	.1854	.4819**	—		
Time 3	-.3129	-.0719	-.1144	-.1588	-.1725	-.2155	-.1289	.0261	.2710	.2843	—	
Total Time	-.4163*	-.0867	-.1569	-.1404	-.2100	-.226	-.1076	.0642	.4745**	.5392**	.9530**	—

** $p < .01$, * $p < .05$

for grade-V *S*s also reveals the same trend i.e., simultaneous measures do not project a strong cluster, nor do successive measures excepting for digit span subscores; but planning measures project a strong cluster. Here also digit span scores did not correlate with planning scores. Thus, across both the grade levels planning factors projected a strong cluster; and they did not show significant relation to any other measure.

Discussion and Conclusion

Table 5.1 shows that at Grade-II level, of all the predictor measures, one of the planning measures determined significantly correct performance at oral reading. Grade-II children happen to be beginning readers who are learning how to read. They have undertaken reading skill acquisition instructions for one year only. Even this group has shown that one of the planning measures contributes significantly to reading performance. This measure was the time taken at trial two of the trail making test.

It may be stated here that the trail making test consisted of three trials with increasing difficulty level. Trial one consisted of few digits and the subjects task here was to connect them sequentially. Trial two consisted of a mixture of few digits and letters distributed randomly and the subject's task here was to start with the first digit then connect it to the first letter, move to the second digit, connect it to the second letter and so on. The third trial also consisted of digits and letters but here the number of digits and letters were much more than they were for second trial. Here also subject's task was the same as it was in case of second trial. Thus the first trial was easiest among the three, while the third trial was most difficult. Probably it was the second trial which was of optimum difficulty level for children of this grade hence could discriminate between good and poor planners. Since planning relates to reading, performance here accounted for significant variance in reading processes.

Grade-V children showed that time taken for third trial of trial making test happens to be the best determiner of oral reading performance. This variable contributed 9.38 per cent of variance in the dependent measure. Next variable was total time taken by subject over all three trials of the trail making test and these two variables taken together contribute 18.40 per cent of variance in the dependent measure. At this grade level the best set of predictors for oral reading, thus, consisted of time taken at third trial of trail making test and total time taken on this test across all three trials. These two variables are planning variables.

Intercorrelations tables show that excepting for planning measures neither simultaneous measures nor successive measures projected a strong cluster. Planning, on the other hand, did not project strong relation to any other process. It was probably for this reason that when marker planning variables were set aside through stepwise regression analyses no other variable came up showing significant additional variance in the predicted measure. This observation too, is significant. It implies that simultaneous, successive and planning processes taken together significantly contribute to oral reading performance; but planning processes make up the marker processes.

The common feature showed by Grade-II and V children is that oral reading performance is determined significantly by planning variables. Oral reading primarily involves decoding of graphemes into the phonic space. This decoding is based on selective perception of significant graphemic content of the text, supplemented by projected expectancies. It does not involve just a passive sequential decoding of graphemes.

The present study used trail making test as the measure of planning. Trail making involves planned visual search. The subject has to visually search through the stimulus field as per a predecided plan. Oral reading which involves selective perception of significant graphemes could be viewed to be a planned visual search activity involving selective perception of significant graphemes. Probably because of this commonality factor between trail making and oral reading the former has come to contribute significantly in the later's variance.

Beta coefficients (see Tables 5.1 and 5.2) for the predictor variables show that these values are negative. It means, lesser time one took to complete the visual search task better he was at oral reading. Time taken at planned visual search and performance on oral reading have been found to be negatively related. This is probably because of the fact that both activities involve planned visual search; hence quicker one is at it better he is at reading.

Studies in the context of English orthography have shown that planning factors contribute to reading processes (Ramey, 1985). Subjects good on visual search performed better than comparable subjects who were poor in visual search on reading tasks and recall of literary passages. Intelligence differences, however, did not exist between good and poor visual searchers. Reading, recall of sentences, inferential statements about the passage were better for the former group.

The present findings in the context of Oriya orthography coroborate observations made in English orthography. This is despite the fact that

Oriya and English orthographies have significantly different features and these differences could lead to different reading strategies. Though English is an alphabetic and non-phonetic orthography and Oriya is a syllabic and phonetic orthography, so far as oral reading is concerned, the commonality between the two is that both orthographies demand a planful visual search.

Thus, the present study shows that oral reading in the context of Oriya orthography is significantly determined by planned visual search processes. This holds good for beginning as well as for fluent oral readers.

Summary

The present study looked into the role of simultaneous-successive scanning and planning processes in oral reading in Oriya Orthography. Subjects (*S*s) were drawn from Grade-II and V. Grade-II *S*s were beginning readers and Grade-V *S*s were fluent oral readers. Sample consisted of 25 boys and 25 girls from each grade. Total sample size was 100. All the *S*s were administered with simultaneous, successive and planning measures, and grade-appropriate oral reading tasks. Results showed that boys and girls did not differ on measures under observation. Data acrose sex groups were pooled together during further analyses. Multiple correlations (Rs) showed that all the measures taken together contribute significant variance in correct oral reading. Stepwise multiple regression analyses showed that of all the predictor measures planning measures made up best set of predictors. Results have been interpreted in the light of the fact that oral reading involves planned visual search through the text.

6

READING ABILITY AND INFORMATION PROCESSING STRATEGIES

Reading is considered as a psycholinguistic process, where the reader processes three kinds of information: graphophonic, syntactic and semantic, as she/he reacts to the graphic display on the page. It is a process in which meaning is attributed to a linguistic medium of communication (Goodman, 1969). Reading, far from being a series of word perceptions, is a selective process involving a partial use of available language cues. It is described as 'a psycholinguistic guessing game'. Efficient reading does not result from precise perception and identification of elements, but from skill in selecting the 'fewest, most productive cues necessary to produce guesses' (Goodman, 1980).

Using Luria's (1966a, 1966b) concept of simultaneous and successive processing, Das, Kirby and Jarman (1975, 1979) proposed a model of information processing. The model assumes that two modes of processing information are available to the individual: simultaneous and successive. Simultaneous processing refers to the synthesis of separate elements into groups in such a way that any portion of the result is at once accessible without dependence upon its position in the whole. Successive processing refers to processing of information in serial order. The individual selects either or both modes of processing, depending upon his or her habitual mode of information processing as determined by socio-cultural and genetic factors, and the demands of the task. Das and Jarman (1981) claim that simultaneous and successive processes are not coexistent with visual and auditory modalities; are not similar to reasoning and memory; and are not similar to verbal and non-verbal factors. They are useful categories of cognitive processes, and are not merely redundant labels. The model of Das *et al.*, has been cross-

---

Co-author Gita Devi

validated by Ryckman (1981) and Naglieri *et al.*, (1981) who used different sets of measures.

Attempts have been made using factor analysis of data from cognitive processing tasks to relate factor structure to reading achievement (Leong, 1980; Richman and Lindgren, 1980). Different cognitive structures have been observed for disabled and non-disabled readers which have been claimed to be independent of the method of extracting factors. Other studies (Cummins and Das, 1977; Kirby and Das, 1977; Mcleod, 1978; Ryckman, 1981) have also attempted to relate reading achievement to information-processing strategies by using simultaneous and successive processing tasks. Results have led to the conclusion that children with different reading abilities process information differently.

Most of these studies used good and poor readers matched for intelligence. But matching for intelligence creates an artificial situation, wherein the real differences/similarities in processing strategies might not show up, especially if their population parameters are really different. Moreover, these studies did not include comparable simultaneous and successive processing tasks. Hence it has not been possible to make within-group comparisons of simultaneous and successive processing abilities. Further, studies taking good and poor readers within the normal reading range are lacking.

Thus, the present study looked into the information processing strategies of good and poor readers who were not matched for intelligence. It was intended to treat the effect of intelligence as a covariate. The study included, along with other measures, two comparable measures of simultaneous and successive processing abilities, and used good and poor readers within the normal reading range.

Method

Sample

The study included good and poor readers of 9 to 11 years of age, with average age of 10.13 years, from grade V of an urban school in Bhubaneswar, Orissa, India. All the 90 students of grade-V were given a reading task, which was devised following Schonell and Schonell's (1955) model. This task contained very simple to very difficult sentences of increasing length. Errors of omission and commission, errors of mispronunciation, failure to stop at commas and full stops, and incorrect stress or emphasis were recorded for each child, yielding total scores for the four types of errors.

In addition, the teacher's rating of each child for reading ability was taken on a five-point scale. It was observed that all the four types of reading errors showed a significant relationship to the teacher's rating. High correlations were noted for the first two types of reading errors and the teacher's rating (r = -0.67, -0.87, df = 88, $p < 0.01$ in both cases). Hence, on of the basis of those two types of errors, all the children were divided into three groups. The 30 highest scorers made up the poor reader group and the 30 lowest made up the good reader group.

Tests used

The figure copying test (Ilg and Ames, 1964) and the serial recall test have been used as measures of simultaneous and successive processing by Das, Kirby and Jarman (1979). Figure copying requires the child to copy 10 geometrical forms which increase in difficulty and are visible to the child at all times. Each drawing is scored as 0, 1 or 2, according to the degree of correctness of reproduction.

In the serial recall task the child is verbally presented with a group of four neutral words. His or her task is to recall verbally, immediately after their presentation, these words in their proper serial position. There are 24 such groups of four words and the maximum score is 96. All the 96 words were given in Oriya (i.e., the mother tongue of the sample).

Apart from the above tasks, the present study included two subtests of the WISC (Gujrati Adaptation, Bhatt, 1973). They were; the test of similarities and the test of digit span (the digit span test was also used by Dàs, Kirby and Jarman, 1979). In the test of similarities, names of two familiar objects are presented to the child, and the child's task is to state how those objects are similar to each other. There are 16 such pairs of object names of increasing difficulty level. Responses are scored 0,1 or 2, depending upon the appropriateness of the response. This test satisfies the requirements of a simultaneous task and was included as a measure of simultaneous processing.

The digit span test requires the child to repeat a series of digits in the way they are presented (i.e., forward digit span) or in the reverse order (i.e. backward digit span). The length of the series is increased from three in the case of forward, and two in the case of backword, upto nine. This test was used as a measure of successive processing that was comparable with the test of similarities when both sets of scores were converted into scaled scores.

Raven's Coloured Progressive Matrices (RPM; Raven, 1965) was used as the non-verbal measure of intelligence. Responses to each item and total time taken to complete RPM were recorded for each child.

Results

It was found that the good reader group had a mean ($\overline{X}$) RPM score of 19.47 and the poor reader group had a $\overline{X}$ score of 19.87. These two groups did not differ significantly on this measure. Mean time taken to complete RPM by good readers was 10.63 (SD = 1.79). For poor reader it was 12.60 (SD = 2.47). These means differed significantly ($t = 3.52$; $df = 29$; $p < .01$).

Between Groups Differences

So far as their scores on simultaneous and successive processing strategies were concerned the good readers had $\overline{X}$ values of 22.40 (similarities - raw score), 17.20 (similarities - scaled score) and 15.20 (figure copying test) with SD values of 6.04, 4.05 and 3.11. Their $\overline{X}$ scores for digit span test and serial recall test were : 9.97 (raw score) and 11.53 (scaled score); and 64.90. Accompanying SD values were: 1.65, 3.33, and 5.40. Poor readers scored 9.40 (similarities - raw score), 8.27 (similarities - scaled score), and 11.77 (figure copying) with SD values of 5.07, 3.88 and 3.53 respectively. This group scored 7.33 (digit span- raw score), 6.33 (digit span- scaled score), and 58.03 (serial recall); with accompanying SD values of 1.75, 3.51 and 9.13. This shows that on all the simultaneous and successive measures the poor reading group scored lower than the good reading group. Though the two groups did not differ significantly on RPM scores an insignificant RPM difference still might have a significant effect on simultaneous and successive processing strategies. Hence analysis of covariance was used to statistically partial out the effect of intelligence on the simultaneous and successive processing scores.

Table 6.1 Presents the results of analyses of covariance for all the simultaneous and successive tasks. This table shows that on all the simultaneous and successive measures the difference between the good and poor readers, which exists in favour of the former group, is significant, after partialling out the effect of intelligence.

Within Groups Differences

In order to assess within groups performances over simultaneous and sucessive tasks, the good reader' scaled scores on the similarities test

TABLE 6.1: Results of analyses of covariance, taking RPM as covariate in each case, for all the simultaneous and successive processing tasks

Soures of Variance	Tests of Simultaneous processing: Test of Similarities: MSV for Raw Scores	Tests of Simultaneous processing: Test of Similarities: MSV for Scaled Scores	Tests of Simultaneous processing: MSV for Figure Copying Scores	Tests of Successive processing: Test of Digit Span: MSV for Raw Scores	Tests of Successive processing: Test of Digit Span: MSV for Scaled Scores	Tests of Successive processing: MSV for Serial Recall Scores
Between Groups (*df* = 1)	2551.90	1230.91	183.30	105.75	412.93	702.62
Within Groups (*df* = 57)	31.56	15.07	10.05	2.78	11.18	57.14
F - ratios	80.85*	78.56*	18.24*	37.99*	36.93*	12.30*

* Significant at 0.01 level

were compared with their scaled scores on the digit span test. The mean difference of 5.70 was in favour of scaled similarities scores. The *t*-ratio was found to be significant ($t = 7.13$, $df = 29$, $p < 0.01$). A similar comparision of poor readers' scaled scores on the similarities test and their scaled scores on the digit span test, with a mean difference of 1.94 in favour of scaled similarities scores, revealed that the *t* - ratio was not significant ($t = 1.78$, $df = 29$, $p > 0.05$). These findings suggest that the good readers are relatively better at simultaneous processing than successive processing, and possess a differentiated processing strategy, whereas the poor readers score equally in both strategies, and appear, therefore, not to possess a differentiated processing strategy.

Discussion

The fact that good and poor readers did not differ on RPM scores, but differed on time taken to complete the task, is interesting. This finding implies that these two groups, though not different in intelligence, are different in the time they take to process visual information. But ultimately both arrive at the same decision. This has significant implications for reading.

The finding that good readers scored significantly higher on stmiultaneous as well as successive measures corroborated previous findings (Cummins and Das, 1977; Kirby and Das, 1977; Mcleod, 1978; Leong, 1980). Das, Kirby and Jarman (1979) concluded that high reading achievement is reserved for those who have relatively high levels of ability in both forms of processing. Leong's (1981) scatter of factor scores shows that the above-average readers tend to cluster in the high simultaneous and high successive quadrant, and below-average readers tend to cluster in the low simultaneaous and low successive quadrant.

When comparision of performance on simultaneous and successive tasks was made within the groups, the good reading group gave a significantly better performance on simultaneous tasks than on sucessive tasks. A similar comparison for the poor reading group did not reveal any significant difference. This observation is revealing and significant. It implies not only that the good reading group generally performed better on both simultaneous and successive processing strategies but also that they had a still better developed simultaneous processing strategy. However, the significance of this differential processing ability for reading achivement is a question which needs probing.

In contrast with the good readers, the poor readers not only had a lower level of simultaneous and successive ability but also gave no sign of differential processing abilities. Whether this undifferentiated strategy of information processing hinders reading achievement is yet to be answered. Present findings suggest that this difference between good and poor readers, with reference to information processing should be explored further.

Summary

Sixty readers (30 good and 30 poor readers) between the age of 9 and 11 years from grade-V in an urban school in Orissa, India, were given simultaneous and successive information-processing tasks, some of which were comparable. They were also tested with Raven's Progressive Matrices (RPM). The two groups did not differ on RPM scores, but the poor reader group took significantly more time to complete the test. This implies a delay in visual scanning for poor readers. Good readers performed better than the poor readers on the simultaneous and successive tasks. When performance in these two tasks within the groups was compared, it was observed that the good readers scored significantly higher in the simultaneous than in the successive tasks, but the poor readers had almost equal scores in simultaneous and successive tasks. This observation points to the importance of simultaneous processing in oral reading.

7

READING COMPREHENSION AND INFORMATION PROCESSING STRATEGIES

Oral reading and reading comprehension make up two different facets of the reading process. Oral reading is primarily concerned with the process of grapheme-to-phoneme conversion; and reading comprehension is concerned with the process of infering the ideas and information that the author intends to convey.

Reading comprehension depends on two factors: one, the information contained in the text, and the other, the background information available with the reader, i.e. the reader's world view. The reader draws inferences from the text supplementing the missing links from his own information background. Thus, comprehension is the outcome of an interaction between these two sources of information.

Information processing strategies refer to the ways in which an individual takes the incoming information. These are mostly the individual's habitual modes of taking-in the information from the outer world. Das, Kirby and Jarman (1979) propose two different ways in which people receive the incoming information: the simultaneous and the successive modes of processing the in-coming information. People who are used to processing information simultaneously make a concurrent scan of all the stimuli coming within their perview. On the other hand, people who process information successively take up one bit at a time, receive and register in the central processing unit, and then go for the next bit. Thus simultaneous and successive scanning processes are two different ways of receiving the incoming information and registering them in the central processing unit for their use in cognitive acts.

Reading, being a cognitive behaviour, relates to the modes of information processing. Kirby and Das (1977) taking fourth-grade boys

---

Co-author Abantika Kar

observed that reading achievement was related to high levels of ability in both forms of processing. Cummins and Das' (1977) study corroborated Kirby and Das' findings and established that simultaneous processing is necessary for the development of more advanced levels of comprehension skills. McLeod (1971) taking children from 4th grade observed that at higher levels of reading competence simultaneous processing is more important than successive processing. Competence in simultaneous processing and in inferencing (based on oral reading) were found to be closely related. Das and Mensinck (1989) using selected simultaneous and sequential tests from the Kaufman Assesment Battery for children (K-ABC) along with a new verbal simultaneous test observe that high simultaneous and sequential scores were associated with reading comprehension. All the above cited studies have been done taking English orthography into account, which is an alphabetic, non-phonetic (Wagner and Torgesen, 1987) type of orthography.

It is possible that different orthographies demand differentiated proficiency in information processing of their readers. So far as oral reading is concerned an alphabetic orthography like English might demand an holistic simultaneous scan from the reader. Because each letter by itself rarely forms a whole word, only combinations of letters produce words. Moreover, phonetic equivalences of letters vary depending upon the word context in which they appear. In such a case the reader cannot take a letter-by-letter reading approach, and still then end up in a correct reading of the word. For a correct word reading the reader has to make a scan or a guess of all the letter contents, the guess being the result of an automatic expectancy process. An holistic word reading strategy is a necessary prerequisite for a correct rendering, which in turn, implies proficiency at simultaneous processing. On the other hand logographic and syllabic orthographies may not demand an holistic word-scan strategy, since in these cases each character is either a meaningful unit or at least a pronounceable unit and character-by-character identification and reading could be sufficient to produce a correct word reading. Hence, proficiency at successive scanning would be sufficient to produce correct reading, while proficiency at simultaneous scanning may not be demanded from the reader.

Moreover, the variance or invariance of grapheme-to-phoneme conversion could bear significant implications for its readers' decoding strategies. When an orthography is phonetic, that is, has almost invariant grapheme-to-phoneme correspondence, phonetic conversion of individual characters may result in correct word reading. Thus, in the case of logographic and syllabic orthographies proficiency at successive scanning would be required for a correct decoding of the print. But, when an orthography is non- phonetic, having poor grapheme-to-phoneme correspondence (as in the case of English orthography) a holistic word scan and/or guess is a necessary prerequisite for a correct decoding. This implies proficiency in simultaneous scanning.

Thus, different orthographies, through their demands at the stage of decoding could be promoting different habits of information processing in their readers. These may not remain confined to oral reading situations only, and may generalize to reading situations involving comprehension.

Oriya orthography, on which the present study is based, is an alphabetic-syllabic type of phonetic orthography, having very good grapheme-to-phoneme correspondence. Studies have been done relating oral reading processes in Oriya orthography to information processing strategies of the reader. Sahu and Devi (1986) took beginning readers from 2nd grade who had started learning to read Oriya orthography. Contrasted groups of good and poor oral readers showed differences in simultaneous and successive processing abilities, and these differences existed in favour of the former group. It was observed that at the beginning stage of reading Oriya orthography, there is probably a greater dependence on successive processing than on simultaneous processing. Sahu and Devi (1984) taking relatively fluent Oriya oral readers observe that proficiency at oral reading goes with better performance at both simultaneous and successive tasks. But, so far as readers' differential proficiency in these strategies was concerned, good readers projected a differentiated strategy in favour of simultaneous processing, but poor readers did not project any differentiated strategy.

The above studies were confined to oral reading and did not probe the relationship between information processing strategies and reading comprehension in Oriya orthography. The present study assessed how reading comprehension is related to the modes of information processing when a reader reads Oriya orthography. It took into account fluent oral readers so as to avoid the interfering effect of jerky oral reading on comprehension. Moreover, the study aimed at statistically partialling out the possible effect of intelligence variance on observations instead of controlling for this at the level of sampling. Drawing sample cases from good and poor comprehender groups matched for intelligence might end up in drawing sample cases from upper strata of one population (stratification being based on intelligence score) and from lower strata of another population, in case population parameters of intelligence are different. This may produce an experimental artifact. Since parametric values of intelligence of good and poor comprehender groups are unknown, it was decided to statistically control the role of intelligence variance at the time of data analysis, instead of doing it at the time of sampling.

Method

Subjects

One hundred children reading in grade-V of two schools of Cuttack, one of the cities of Orissa, India, served as the subjects (*S*s) for the present study. Oriya was the mother tongue as well as the medium of instruction in school for all the *S*s. The sample consisted of almost equal number of male and female *S*s. The mean ($\overline{X}$) age of the sample was 117 months with a standard deviation (SD) value of 3.69.

The Nature of Oriya Orthography

All writing systems can be broadly divided into three categories, i.e. logographic alphabetic and syllabic types of orthographies (Taylor, 1981). Oriya orthography has the characteristic features of both the syllabic type of orthography and the alphabetic type of orthography. It consists of 47 letters of which 12 are vowels and 35 are consonants. Each letter has a name and the letter name happens to be the phonic sound of the letter. The phonic sound of the letter remains constant across all types of use of the letter. Hence the grapheme-phoneme correspondence is almost invariant in Oriya orthography. Thus, Oriya is an alphabetic-syllabic type of phonetic orthography.

Also, the vowel sounds in the Oriya orthography could be symbolically added to the consonants and these symbols are called *matras.* The addition of *matra* slightly changes the phonic sound of the consonant in the direction of the vowel represented by the symbol. Besides, the phonic sounds of a few consonants could be symbolically presented called *phalas. Phalas* could be added to other consonants, and in such a case the phonic sound of the character is a combination of the phonetic representations of both the consonants. Moreover, a few consonants could be combined together to make a single character called a *yuktakshyara.* The phonic sound of a *yuktakshyara,* as in case of addition of a *phala* to a consonant, retains the phonic representations of constituent consonants. Consonants with *phala* and *yuktakshyara* could be viewed as conjunct consonants. The wide possibility of making various combinations with the help of *matras, phalas* and *yuktakshyaras* go to enrich the orthography; and with accompanying meaning variations, go to enrich the language. But, this very source of orthopgraphic and language enrichment makes Oriya writing difficult and reading complicated.

Tasks and Tests Used

1. *Reading Comprehension Tests*

The present study used both cloze and passage comprehension tasks to assess reading comprehension.

The Cloze task: The present study used the cloze tasks developed by Sahu and Mishra (1988). The task consists of two short stories of 118 and 157 word length, with every eighth word deleted. Hence there were 14 deletions in the first story and 19 deletions in the second story. The subject was to go through the mutilated story once, and then suggest possible words for the deletions. Two stories were administered one after the other. Time taken by the subject to read the story with deletions and his responses for the deletions were recorded.

Each correct response got a score of one. *S*'s number of correct responses, incorrect responses, and number of failures to respond were scored.

The Passage Comprehension Task: In the present study, two short stories of 282 and 238 word length were selected. For each story 16 questions (eight literal and eight inferential comprehension) were formulated. Then a pilot testing was done on 10 students. All the 10 students were asked to read the stories and to answer the questions. Final selection of question were done on the basis of their difficulty levels. Very easy and very difficult questions were dropped out and questions within 20 per cent to 80 per cent success range were retained. In this process 10 questions for each story were finally selected. Out of these 10, five belonged to the literal comprehension group of questions; and five belonged to the inferential comprehension group of questions. Correct answer to each question got one score.

2. *Information Processing Tests*

Tests of Simultaneous Processing

Test of Similarities: This was a sub-test of Gujarati adaptation of the

Wechsler Intelligence Scale for Children (Bhatt, 1973). Translations into Oriya and necessary reordering of items had been done after a pilot testing (Sahu, 1978). This translated and re-ordered version was administered on the present sample. The scoring procedure was not changed.

Figure Copying test: The figure copying test was originally developed by Ilg and Ames (1964) to determine developmental readiness for traditional school-learning tasks of the primary school children. This test has been used as one of the marker tests of simultaneous processing by Das *et al.* (1979). The test requires the subject to copy ten geometrical forms arranged in increasing order of difficulty. Each of 10 drawings is scored as 0,1 and 2 according to the degree of correctness of reproduction. The scoring criteria emphasize the maintenance of geometric relations and proportions rather than exact reproductions.

Tests of Successive Processing

Digit-span test: This is one of the subscales of the Wechsler Intelligence Scale for Children. Both forward and backward series were administered on the present sample.

Serial recall test: Nineteen lists of four words were verbally presented to the subject. After the presentation of each list the subject was immediately required to recall in the correct serial order, as many of the words as he could. The score of the subject was the number of items recalled in proper order. This test has been used as a test of sucessive processing by Das *et al.* (1979).

Similarities and digit-span subscales of Bhatt's Gujarati adaptation of WISC were selected among simultaneous and successive measures with the intention that after conversion into scaled scores, the scores across these tests become directly comparable. WISC subtests have widely varying test items and credit points, and as such, performance on these subtests are not directly comparable. Scaled scores are transformed raw scores with specified mean and standard deviation parameters for all subtests. Raw scores are converted into scaled scores in order to have comparable subtest scores. Conversion is done with the help of age-specific conversion tables given in the test manual. So, in order to make within-groups comparision across processing strategies possible, similarities and digit span subtests of WISC were selected.

3. *Intelligence Test*

Raven's Colour Progressive Matrices (RCPM) was administered as the non-verbal test of intelligence on the present sample.

Passage Comprehension test, figure copying test and RCPM were administered in small groups of four to five *S*s each. All other measures were individually administered.

Results

The mean age of *S*s was 117 (months), So far as their performance on cloze task was concerned the $\overline{X}$s for correct and incorrect responses were 13.89 and 14.25. The same value for failure responses was 5.29. On passage comprehension task $\overline{X}$ values for correct literal and inferential comprehension scores were: 5.98 and 5.53. These values for simultaneous and successive processing tasks were: 14.18 (similarity – raw scores i.e. RS), 12.89 (similarity – scaled score SS), 13.73 (figure copying, FC), 11.04 (digit span – raw score, DSRS), 13.64 (digit span – scaled score, DSSS), and 64.84 (serial recall, SR). Mean RCPM score was 21.85. In order to see if two measures of comprehension correlate between themselves Pearson's coefficients of correlations were obtained between them. It was observed that correct cloze responses correlate significantly with literal comprehension (r = .67, df = 98, p < .01); inferential comprehension (r = .38, df = 98, p < .01), and both literial and inferential comprehension taken together (r = .46, df = 98, p < .01) though the magnitude of correlations differed widely. These findings imply that both the measures of comprehension (i.e. cloze and passage comprehension) correlate significantly; but cloze correlates better with the literal comprehension aspect of passage comprehension than with its inferential comprehension. This suggests that probably cloze, literal comprehension and inferential comprehension assess different facets of reading comprehension.

Cloze Performance and Information Processing

In order to see how cloze performance is related to information processing, two contrasting groups of relatively good and poor cloze task performers were formed. This was done by taking subjects who scored relatively high i.e., 16 to 24 on cloze tasks in the group of good comprehenders (as defined by their cloze task performance); and the subjects who scored relatively low i.e., 5 to 11 in the group of poor comprehenders (as defined by their cloze task performance). There were 34 subjects in each of these two groups. The good and poor comprehenders scored (i.e. $\overline{X}$s) 18.91 and 9.08 as cloze correct responses. Their scores on simultaneous tests were : 19.88 and 11.15 (RS); 16.47 and 10.29 (SS); and 15.56 and 12.91 (FC). On successive measures scores were : 12.74 and 10.21 (DS-RS); 16.26 and 12.32 (DR-SS); and 70.24 and 62.38 (SR). RCPM values were: 27.35 and 18.18. The RCPM scores of good and poor comprehenders showed wide difference in favour of the former group. A '*t*' test showed the difference was statistically significant ($t = 8.04$, $df = 66$, $p < .01$).

Between-Groups Comparison

A significant mean difference on RCPM necessitated statistical partialling of RCPM variance during further analyses while comparing good and poor comprehenders for their inmformation processing strategies. This was done by applying analysis of covariance (Winer, 1971).

Tables 7.1 (a) and 7.1 (b) present the results of tests of significance of mean differences between good and poor comprehenders through the application of analyses of covariance. These tables show that even after partialling out the RCPM effect, mean differences on simultaneous and successive processing tasks, which existed in favour of the good comprehender group, were retained. This established that good comprehenders were better simultaneous and successive processors, abstraction and reasoning being held constant.

Within-Groups Comparison

Again, to see the relative proficiency of each of these groups at simultaneous and successive processing strategies within-groups comparisons were done. This was done for the scaled scores of similarities and digit span subtests, not for other measures of simultaneous and successive processing. Of all the measures taken into account in the present study only scaled score of similarities subtest (as a simultaneous processing score) is comparable with the scaled score of digit span subtest (as a successive processing score). Other measures of simultaneous and sucessive processing were not comparable, hence such comparisons were not done.

Mean differences on similarities and digit span scaled scores were not significant ($p > .05$). For both the comprehender groups t value were .59 ($df = 66$) and 1.78 ($df = 33$) respectively (for good and poor

TABLE 7.1(a): Summaries of analyses of covariance for simultaneous information processing strategies (RCPM covariate in each case) tests of simultaneous processing

	Similarities								Figure copying			
	Raw Score				Scaled Score							
Sources of variances	SS	*df*	MS	*F*	SS	*df*	MS	*F*	SS	*df*	MS	*F*
Total	1254.47	66	—	23.27 $p < .01$	554.12	16	—	11.48 $p < .01$	342.04	66	—	56.55 $p < .01$
Error	923.76	65	14.21	—	470.40	65	7.24	—	341.93	65	6.22	—
Treatment	330.71	1	330.71	—	83.12	1	83.12	—	.11	1	.11	—

TABLE 7.1(b): Summaries of analyses of covariance for successive information processing strategies (RCPM covariate in each case) tests of successive processing

	Digit Span								Serial Recall			
	Raw Score				Scaled Score							
Sources of variances	SS	*df*	MS	*F*	SS	*df*	MS	*F*	SS	*df*	MS	*F*
Total	395.56	66	—	7.02 $p < .05$	593.66	66	—	16.84 $p < .01$	3780.73	66	—	4.22 $p < .01$
Error	357	65	5.49	—	482	65	6.59	—	3550.28	65	54.62	—
Treatment	38.56	1	38.56	—	111.66	1	111.66	—	230.45	1	230.45	—

comprehenders). This establishes that none of the groups had differential proficiency in any one mode of processing information.

Passage Comprehension Performance and Information Processing

In order to see how passage comprehension performance is related to information processing, two contrasting groups of relatively good and poor passage comprehension task performers were formed. This was done by taking subjects who scored relatively high,i.e. 14 to 19, on the passage comprehension task in the group of good comprehenders (as defined by their passage comprehension task performance); and the subjects who scored relatively low i.e., 0 to 10 in the group of poor comprehenders (as defined by their passage comprehension task performance). There were 34 subjects in each of these two group. Good and poor comprehenders had $\overline{X}$ values of 15.26 and 6.47 on passage comprehension task. Their $\overline{X}$ scores on simultaneous tests were : 17.44 and 11.15 (Sim-RS), 14.94 and 10.50 (Sim-SS); and 14.94 and 12.74 (FC). On successive tests they scored: 11.74 and 9.44 (DS-RS), 14.38 and 11.76 (DS-SS) and 66.68 and 61.71 (SR). On RCPM these values were 26.12 and 18.71. The RCPM scores of good and poor comprehenders showed a significant difference in favour of the former group ($t = 5.29$, $df = 66$, $p < .05$).

Between-Groups Comparison

A significant mean difference on RCPM necessitated statistical partialling of its variance during further analyses while comparing good and poor comprehenders for their information processing. This was done by applying analysis of covariance (Winer, 1971).

Tables 7.2 (a) and 7.2 (b) present the results of tests of significance of mean differences between good and poor comprehenders through the application of analyses of covariance.

Tables 7.2 (a) and 7.2 (b) show that even after partialling out the RCPM effect, mean differences, which existed in favour of the good comprehender group were statistically significant, excepting for figure copying and digit span scaled scores and similarities scores. This established that good comprehenders were better off on simultaneous and successive information tasks.

Within-Groups' Comparison

Again to examine the relative proficiency of each of these groups on simultaneous and successive processing strategies, within groups comparisons were done. Here also the comparision was made between the scaled scores of similarities subtest and the scaled scores of digit-span subtest for reasons already stated. Mean differences on scaled measures of similarities and digit-span tests were not significant ($p > .05$) for both good and poor comprehender groups; t values were .59 ($df = 66$) and 1.41 (df=33) respectively. This establishes that none of these groups showed differential proficiency in any one mode of processing information.

Reading Comprehension and Information Processing

Results reported up to now show how reading comprehension, as defined by any one of the measures, relates to information processing. As has already been pointed out, these measures probably assess reading comprehension from different angles, and hence end up assessing different facets of it. Proficiency at reading comprehension, as defined by both the measures taken together, would be more reliable.

In order to generate good and poor comprehenders, taking both the measures of comprehension into account, a double-median-split technique taking cloze and passage comprehension scores was followed. This divided the whole sample into four groups on the basis of their cloze and passage comprension scores; the good-good group; the good-poor group; the poor good group and the poor-poor group. Performance of the good-good group was compared with the performance of the poor-poor group of subjects. Hereafter, these two groups are referred to as the good and poor comprehender groups respectively. There were 35, subjects in the good and 29 subjects in the poor comprehender group. The good comprehender group had $\overline{X}$ values of 18.60 and 13.97 on cloze task and passage comprehension task. Comparable scores for poor comprehenders were: 10.62 and 5.93. The two groups had 19.54 and 10.28 as Sim-RS values; 15.89 and 10.03 as Sim-SS values, 15.31 and 11.90 as FC values. Values for DS-RS were 12.83 and 9.62; DS-SS were 16.57 and 11.24; and for SR they were 70.11, and 61.07. On RCPM these two groups scored 26.83 and 17.31.

Since RCPM differences between good and poor comprehenders showed wide difference in favour of the former group, a 't' test was

TABLE 7.2 (a): Summeries of analyses of covariance for simultaneous information processing strategies (RCPM covariate in each case)

tests of simultaneous processing

Sources of	Similarities								Figure Copying			
	Raw Score				Scaled Score							
Variances	SS	*df*	MS	*F*	SS	*df*	MS	*F*	SS	*df*	MS	*F*
Total	1198.62	66	—	4.42	621.43	66	—	4.95	676.56	66	—	1.02
				$p < .05$				$p <. 05$				p>.05
Error	1122.28	65	17.27	—	577.51	65	8.88	—	666.08	65	10.24	—
Treatment	76.34	1	76.34	—	43.92	1	43.92	—	10.48	1	10.48	—

TABLE 7.2 (b): Summaries of analysis of coariance for successive information processing strategies (RCPM covariate in each case)

tests of successive information processing

Sources of	Digit span								Serial Recall			
	Raw Score				Scaled Score							
variances	SS	*df*	MS	*F*	SS	*df*	MS	*F*	SS	*df*	MS	*F*
Total	160.77	66	—	13.29	921.05	66	—	.22	4084.24	66	—	.05
				$p <. 01$				$p > .05$				$p > .05$
Error	133.53	65	2.05	—	917.91	65	14.12	—	4080.91	65	62.77	—
Treatment	27.24	1	27.24	—	3.15	1	3.15	—	3.05	1	3.05	—

done. The '*t*' ratio was found to be statistically significant (t =9.52, df= 64, p < .01).

Between-Groups Comparison

Tables 7.3 (a) and 7.3 (b) present the results of tests of significance of mean differences between good and poor comprehenders through analyses of covariance, with RCPM scores being the covariate.

Here again, the good comprehender group excelled their poor comprehender counterparts on all the measures of simultaneous and successive processing tasks, except for figure copying, even after the RCPM effect was partialled out.

Within-Group Comparison

The scaled scores of similarities and digit-span subtests obtained by each group were compared, to see the relative proficiency of these groups on the processing strategies. The '*t*' ratios for good and poor comprehender groups were .88 (df = 34, p > .05) and 1.44 (df = 28, p > .05), which were not significant, implying that none of the groups showed special proficiency in any one mode of processing information.

Discussion and Conclusion

General Observation

Intercorrelations between cloze, literal and inferential comprehension, though significant, were widely different. This implies that cloze, literal comprehension and inferential comprehension assess text comprehension from different angles. Cloze and passage comprehension could be used as complementary measures of reading comprehension; and use of both the measures might prove to be more reliable than use of any one of them.

The present study used RCPM as a non-verbal measure of intelligence. It was found that good and poor comprehenders differ significantly on the measure of intelligence and this difference was invariably in favour of the former group. Probably this is due to the fact that a child who is better at abstraction and reasoning is capable of holding different bits of information in the short-term storage and is capable of using them more effectively when required. This ability shows up in terms of better reading comprehension performance.

TABLE 7.3 (a): Summaries of analyses of covariance for simultaneous information processing strategies. (RCPM covariate in each case).

test of simultaneous processing

Sources of		Similarities								Figure Copying			
		Raw Score			Scaled Score					Raw Score			
variances	SS	*df*	MS	*F*	SS	*df*	MS	*F*	SS	*df*	MS	*F*
Total	1151.18	62	—	35.18	720	62	—	35.23	551.36	62	—	.13
				$p < .01$				$p < .01$				$p > .05$
Error	730.03	61	11.97	—	456.46	61	7.48	—	550.21	61	9.02	—
Treatment	421.15	1	421.15	—	263.53	1	263.53	—	1.15	1	1.15	—

TABLE 7.3 (b): Summeries of analyses of covariance for successive information processing strategies (RCPM covatiate in each case)

tests of successive processing

Sources of		Digit Span							Serial Recall			
		Raw Score			Scaled Score				Raw Score			
variances	SS	*df*	MS	*F*	SS	*df*	MS	*F*	SS	*df*	MS	*F*
Total	438.59	62	—	22.69	1053.24	62	—	21.40	3920.00	62	—	15.78
				$p < .01$				$p < .01$				$p < .01$
Error	319.69	61	5.24	—	779.65	61	12.78	—	3114.54	61	51.06	—
Treatment	118.90	1	118.90	—	273.59	1	273.59	—	805.46	1	805.46	—

Reading Comprehension in Oriya Orthography and Information Processing

Raven's Colour Progressive Matrices test is widely used as a nonverbal test of intelligence. This test has also been used by Das *et al.* (1979) as a test of simultaneous processing. This means that the test, apart from loading on abstract reasoning, also loads on simultaneous processing. The present study used the test as a measure of intelligence. Tables 7.1 (a) and 7.1 (b), 7.2 (a) and 7.2 (b), and 7.3 (a) and 7.3 (b) show that the superiority of the good over the poor comprehender group in simultaneous and successive processing measure were retained even after the RCPM effect was partialled out though in some cases they did not reach the significance level. This would mean that the good comprehender group would continue performing better than the poor comprehender group on both simultaneous and successive measures even after we equate them on abstract reasoning; and also to some extent on simultaneous processing. This is both interesting and revealing.

The study also tried to determine whether any of the comprehension groups showed any special profficiency over any processing mode. This was done by making within-groups comparisons for comparable simultaneous and successive processing scores. As has already been pointed out no such differential proficiency was located for any of these groups of subjects. However, differential proficiency may emerge with higher comprehension levels than is the case with the present *S*s.

All the above observations have been made in the context of Oriya orthography reading. Good comprehenders of text written in Oriya possess better simultaneous and successive processing abilities than their poor counterparts. This difference is sustained even after abstract reasoning ability and a part of simultaneous processing ability is partialled out. This means that text comprehension in Oriya by grade-V level demands proficiency in both the processing modes.

It was expected that Oriya, being an alphabetic syllabic type of phonetic orthography, might be promoting successive scanning during reading (rationale already stated). But the study did not reveal such a trend. Thus, it can be concluded that reading comprehension in Oriya orthography by grade-V level does not demand special proficiency in any one mode of information processing.

Summary

The present study investigated the relationship between reading comprehension and information processing strategies of relatively fluent oral readers of Oriya orthography. The study was necessary, because Oriya orthography has some significant differences from English orthography and these differences could bear implications for the reading strategies and processess. Hence, it was envisaged that findings in the field of reading research using English orthography may not hold good for the readers of Oriya orthography.

One hundred students of grade-V were taken as subjects in the present study. Reading comprehension tasks, simultaneous and successive information processing tasks, and a non-verbal measure of intelligence were administered to all the subjects.

Results show that good comprehenders were relatively more intelligent than the poor comprehenders. So far as their performance on simultaneous and successive information processing strategies were concerned good comprehenders were better off on both types of coding tasks and these differences were found to be statistically significant in most cases even after the effect of intelligence was partialled out. However, no differential proficiency on either of these coding strategies was observed, neither for the good nor for the poor comprehender group.

8

WORKING MEMORY CAPACITY AND READING IN ORIYA ORTHOGRAPHY

Reading refers to deciphering the meaning from a printed text. The process starts with the visual input from the print, and in interaction with the knowledge background of the reader, ends with the reader arriving at the meaning of the text. Reading process has different facets: oral reading, and reading comprehension. Oral reading is basically decoding the text into its phonemic components. Reading comprehension, on the other hand, is basically decoding the text into its semantic components. There exists controversy as to whether oral reading includes comprehensions or not. Danks and Fears (1979) propose that oral reading may or may not involve comprehension. It depends upon the processes they involve; which in turn, are reader and task dependent. Hence, neither decoding only nor comprehension only rather decoding-cum-comprehension proposition holds good all the time so far as reading is concerned. Researchers have proposed of various factors being the determiners and/or concomitants of reading proficiency. The important ones include cerebral assymetry (Kershner, 1977; Naylor, 1980; Hynd and Semrud-Clickeman, (1989); phonological factors (Pratt and Brady, 1988; Raz and Bryant, 1990); memory factors and linguistic factors (Jorm, 1983; Torgesen and Houck, 1980). A critical review of literature implicates at the validity of linguistic and memory factors in reading (Moore, Kagan, Sahl, and Grant,1982).

So far as role of memory factors in reading is concerned, observations have showed the role of short-term memory in it (More, Kagan, Sahl, and Grant, 1982; Ellis, 1990). Digit span and letter span performances have been shown to be positively related to the level of reading proficiency (Baddley, Thompson, and Buchanan, 1975; Moore,

---

Co-author Sanjita Mishra

Kagan, Sahl and Grant,1982).

Danneman and Carpenter (1980) proposed of a positive relationship between working memory and reading. Working memory is assumed to have both processing and storage functions; serves as the site for executing processes and storing the product of these processes (Baddly and Hitch, 1977; La Berge and Samuels, 1974). Working memory covers a time span of approximately 10 to 15 minutes. Verbal and non-verbal measures of working memory have been developed (Danneman and Carpenter,1980; Seigel and Ryan, 1989; Danneman and Green, 1986).

Researches showing the relationship between working memory capacity; reading proficiency; and spelling ability (Danneman and Carpenter, 1980; Ormrod and Cochran, 1988) have been done mostly in the context of English orthography. English is an alphabetic type of non-phonetic orthography. Since reading different orthographies leads to qualitatively different phonological representations (Besner, 1990), thereby possibly making differential demands on the reader's working memory capacity; researches in the context of other orthographies are needed in order to draw general conclusions about the relationship between working memory and reading. The present study aimed to see the relationship between working memory capacity and reading proficiency in the context of Oriya orthography. Oriya is an alphabetic-syllabic type of phonetic orthography and the language is an officially recognised language of the Government of India.

Method

Problem

The present research aimed to find out the relationship between working memory capacity and reading proficiency of fluent oral readers. This study was conducted in the context of Oriya language and orthography; and took into account both the oral reading and reading comprehension facets of the reading process. Fluent oral readers were taken as subjects (*S*s) so as to avoid the impact of jerky oral reading on comprehension. A note on the nature of Oriya orthography is necessary in order to visualise the implications of this orthography for reading strategies.

Nature of Oriya Orthography

Oriya is one of the officially recognised languages of India. This is the regional language of the State of Orissa. The language has its own script. It consists of 47 alphabets out of which 12 are vowels and 25 are consonants. The typical pattern of writing Oriya consists of making a smaller circle with a bigger circle on the top of it and characteristic letter features marked on either or both the circles.

Besides 47 alphabets, the orthography contains characters marked by symbolic addition of vowel or consonants to some other consonants. They are *matras, phalas, yuktakshyaras* and doubled letters (Praharaj, 1936; Padhi, 1971). A *matra* consists of adding a vowel sign, symbolically to a consonant. A *phala* consists of adding a consonant sign symbolically to another consonant. A *yuktakshyara* is a compound consonant; a composite character with more than one consonant contained in it. Doubled letters are consonants being doubled in order to make a single character. *Phalas, matras, yuktakshyaras* and doubled letters slightly change the phonetic representation of the basic consonant retaining its original phonetic representation to a great extent.

Oriya orthography is alphabetic in the sense that, it consists of several alphabets and each alphabet stands for a phoneme. Secondly, the orthography is syllabic in the sense that each letter is prounciable by and of itself. And the orthography is phonetic in the sense that the grapheme-phoneme correspondence is very good and almost invariant across all usage. Thus, Oriya orthography can be viewed to be an alphabetic-syllabic type of phonetic orthography.

Design

The study aimed to take high and low working memory subject groups from grade-V as the final sample. They were selected from an initial sample of 100 *S*s drawn randomly from one of the schools of Bhubaneswar, the capital city of Orissa. Initial sample and selection of final sample have been described in detail in the section of sample selection. The final sample was administered with oral reading task, reading comprehension task, and a non-verbal test of intelligence. The test of intelligence is included so as to nullify its effect on the dependent measures statistically, if needed.

Tests and Tasks

The following tests and tasks were used in the study.

Tests of Working Memory

Verbal and non-verbal tests of working memory capacity were used in this study. The verbal test of working memory was a reading span test, constructed in Oriya following Danneman and Charpenter's (1980) model.

In case of working memory-language test, subjects had to read a series of sentences aloud at their own pace and recall the last word of each sentence. The test was constructed with 60 unrelated sentences, 13 to 16 words in length, each sentence ended with a different word. Each sentence was typed on a single line across the centre of an 8x5 inch index card. The cards were arranged in three sets of two, three, four, five and six sentences. Blank cards were inserted to mark the beginning and end of each set.

The experimenter showed one card at a time to the subject. The subject was required to read the sentence aloud. As soon as the sentence was read, a second card was placed on top of the first and subject read the new sentence. This procedure was repeated until a blank card signalled that a trial had ended and that he was to recall the last word of each of the sentence in the order in which they had occurred. Subjects were given practice items at the two-sentence level before the test began. They were warned to expect the number of sentences per sets to increase during the course of the test. The span test contained of 3 sets each of two, three, four, five and six sentences. Subjects were presented increasingly longer sets of sentences until they failed on all 3 sets. Testing was terminated at that point. The level at which a subject was correct on two out of three sets was taken as a measure of the subject's reading span.

Non-verbal test of working memory was constructed following Case, Kurland and Goldberg's (1982) model. It involved counting yellow dots from a field of blue and yellow dots arranged in a randomly determined irregular pattern on a 5x8 inch index card for sets of two, three, four or five cards and then recalling the counts for each level. There were three items at each level. None of the *S*s experienced any difficulty in counting dots. Task administration was stopped when the child failed at all the items at one level.

Reading Tasks

Oral reading task and cloze tasks were used in the present study. Oral reading tasks developed by Sahu and Pattnaik (1987) for grade-V was used in the present study. The task consisted of 34 sentences to be read loudly while the experimenter recorded *S*'s performance on a separate sheet. Number of words read correctly, incorrectly were being recorded along with omission and addition of words during reading, and *S*'s complete failure to read words. This task has been shown to be reasonably reliable and valid.

Cloze tasks were used to assess *S*'s reading comprehension. Cloze paragraphs developed by Sahu and Mishra (1989) were used in the present study. The paragraphs had every eighth word deleted from it and the *S*'s task was to suggest possible words for the places of deletion. Suggested words which exactly tallied with the words deleted were taken as correct responses.

Raven's Colour Progressive Matrices

This test was used as a non-verbal measure of intelligence. Each *S*'s responses and the time taken to complete the task were being recorded.

Sample Slection

The initial sample for the study consisted of 100 children drawn from grade-V of one of the primary schools of Bhubaneswar. All these *S*s were administered with language and non-language tests of working memory. Each *S*'s score on each of these tests were then converted into correrponding *Z* scores. These *Z* scores were then summed and a pooled *Z* score was arrived at for each *S*. These pooled *Z* scores varied from +5.26 to -3.12. These *Z* scores were then serially arranged and the top 35 *S*s with high pooled *Z* scores and bottom 35 *S*s with low pooled *Z* scores were taken as high and low-working memory groups of subjects for present study. The high-working memory group (N =35) had mean scores of 3.03 and 3.06 on language and non-language tests of working memory with accompanying, .03 and .33 values as standard deviations. Their pooled *Z* scores ranged from +5.26 to +1.08. The low-working memory group (N = 35) had mean scores of 2.20 and 2.40 on language and non-language tests of working memory with accompanying .16 and .49 values as standard deviations. Their pooled *Z* scores ranged from -0.97 to -3.12.

Results

Mean ($\bar{X}$) correct and incorrect oral reading scores of high working memory group were 395.03 and 3.82 with accompanying standard deviation values of 0.30 and 2.75. For low working memory group the correct and incorrect oral reading scores were 390.49 and 4.57, with SD values of 2.74 and 2.02. For cloze responses the former group had 22.71, 13.77 and 7.51 as $\overline{X}$ correct, incorrect but acceptable, and incorrect and unacceptable responses. These $\overline{X}$s had SD values of 3.69, 5.46, and 2.34. The low working memory group had $\overline{X}$ values of 10.54, 10.54, and 19.00 for the above three categories of responses with SD values of 2.88, 2.88, and 4.07. The mean Raven's Coloured Progressive Matrices (RCPM) scores of high and low-working memory groups were 14.97 and 7.86 respectively with accompanying standard deviation values of 3.73 and .89. RCPM difference was significant (t = 10.95; df = 34; $p < .01$). Since the two groups differed significantly on the measures of intelligence, further analyses necessitated analyses of covariance taking RCPM score as the covariate in order to statistically nullify its effect on the dependent measures, while looking for the difference between these two groups on such measures.

Since the two groups differed on the measures of oral reading and reading comprehension, significance of differences were assessed through analyses of covariance with RCPM as the covariate in each case.

Table 8.1 Shows that the two groups differed significantly on the correct scores of the oral reading task and correct and unacceptable scores of cloze task.

Discussion and Conclusion

Performance on RCPM

The high and low-working memory groups differed significantly on an abstract measure of intelligence. Though, this was not expected, this could have happened for the fact that the high working memory group was capable of retaining all the information, while manipulating with them at the ideational level, since the beginning of the stimulus input till the elicitation of response. This might have helped them to come up with the most appropriate alternative out of all alternative answers given, and inturn, might have raised their scores on this test.

Performance on Reading Tasks

Significant difference on the correct scores for oral reading task and cloze task, this difference being in favour of the high-working memory group, means that high-working memory capacity goes with better reading performance. This difference in favour of high-working memory group is retained, even after the effect of intelligence was nullified, which

TABLE 8.1: Analyses of covariance performed on oral reading and cloze task scores

Sources of Variance	df	Oral Reading Scores				Cloze Scores					
		Correct		Incorrect		Correct		Acceptable		Un-acceptable	
		F ratio	*p* level	*F* ratio	*p* level	*F* ratio	*p* level	*F* ratio	*p* level	*F* ratio	*p* level
Error	67										
		15.72**	<.01	1.26	>.05	21.05**	<.01	0.61	>.05	6.91*	<.05
Treatment	66										

** $p < .01$

* $p < .05$

means that this difference is not due to intelligence difference, but is rather due to or a concomitant of high working memory capacity.

These findings imply that even with an alphabetic-syllabic type of phonetic orthography like Oriya, working memory capacity facilitates both decoding and comprehension processes.

Oriya orthography, like Japanese, is syllabic in nature. Hence, Oriya orthography so far as phonological code is concerned, is probably more closely tied to articulatory activity, than it would be for alphabetic English. But inspite of these possible phonological code differences used for lexical access, the present study shows that high working memory capacity facilitates reading processes in Oriya orthography, as it does in case of English orthography. This is probably due to the fact that working memory serves for both a short period storage-cum-processing site, hence, facilitates reading processes inspite of orthographic variations.

Summary

Working memory capacity has been shown to be related to reading proficiency. Most of these researches have been done in the context of English orthography, an alphabetic type of non-phonetic orthography. Different orthographies elicit different phonological codes for lexical access. The present study was done in the context of Oriya orthography which is an alphabetic—syllabic type of phonetic orthography. The study aimed to locate if working memory capacity goes with reading proficiency. Both oral reading and reading comprehension processes were taken into account.

Fluent oral readers from grade-V were administered with working memory (language nad non-language) measures: oral reading and cloze tasks; and Raven's Colour Progressive Matrics. High and low working memory groups were generated on the basis of their pooled Z scores on both the measures of working memory. Results showed that high working memory group performs better than their low counterparts on oral reading and reading comprehension even when, intelligence effect is statistically partialled out. Findings have been discussed in the light of the nature of working memory; and reading task demands as cognitive tasks.

9

WHAT DOES IT MEAN TO BE HIGH VERBAL ?

Language and cognition are interrelated and interdependent processes. Though they emerge and develop as independent processes, yet, after a particular point of development they interact and influence one another. (Vygotsky, 1962; Piaget, 1955; Kohlberg, Yager and Hjertholm, 1968).

Cognitive abilities are determined by an array of factors; language abilities are probably one of them. So far as the possible role of language in cognition is concerned, it can be visualised that language plays four major functions in this context. One, it probably directs *S*s' attention towards specific aspect or aspects of the stimulus complex; thus, has a regulatory function to perform in the information seeking process. This, in its turn, determines information input, their reception and organization. Information and stimulation do not come in singular ways, they come in arrays, they appear in complexes. For a correct or appropriate performance under a problem situation the *S* has to look for appropriate information from the stimuli presented. Language can be viewed to be playing a significant role at this point of cognitive operation,. The very process of naming and labelling directs *S*s' attention to specific aspects of the stimulus complex, hence stimulus complex gets organised differently for different *S*s to start with. For example, presented with a number of wooden blocks of different geometrical shapes, sizes and colours one child may see them as triangular and squar blocks; another child may see them as big and small blocks; and a third child may see them as red and green blocks, because the first looked for the shape, second for the size; and the third for the colour, being guided by the name or label he used while scanning the blocks. Language, naming and labelling, to be specific, plays a directive and regulatory role in the

---

Co-author Puspa Dash

information search, input, and reception processes. With this, the stimulus complex of the outer world stand organised and categorised; the second probable role of language in cognitive functions. Language, thus, might be determining organization and categorization of stimuli; and conceptualisation and abstraction processes. The third role of language probably consists of storing the concepts and abstracts in long-term memory (LTM). Long-term-memory is semantic in nature (Cowan, 1988). It does not store the details, stores abstractions. Mapping concepts into LTM is facilitated by abstractions through language. The fourth role of language in cogntive functions probably consists of retrieval of abstractions from LTM for concurrent use. The linguistic label assigned for an abstraction retrieves the abstract idea from LTM storage which then is used for solving another problem at hand. Thus, language can be viewed to be playing directive, organising, coding, and retrieval functions during cognitive functions. Viewed thus, if language can be assumed to facilitate cognitive operation, *S*s high on verbal skills can be expected to perform better than *S*s with low verbal skills even on cognitive tasks that weigh primarily on non-language skills.

A sharp distinction between language-based and non-language tests of cognition is not possible, but cognitive tasks that load high on language and linguistic skills; and cognitive tasks that load high on other-than-language and linguistic skills is possible. The former tasks can be grossly labelled as language-based measures of cognition and the latter as non-language measures of cognition. The present study aimed to look into the performance of primary school children of high and low verbal abilities on non-language measures of cognition.

While looking into the non-language cognitive performances of high and low verbal groups, it is possible that intelligence factor may play a confounding role, in case the groups differ on it. This confounding effect can be controlled in two ways i.e. at the level of sampling; and at the level of data analysis. Controlling for intelligence at sample selection level involves taking high and low verbal *S*s of matched intelligence score. But, this method may lead to a methodological error of taking selected, not random sample cases, from both the groups of *S*s in case their population parameters on intelligence are different. Thus, if high verbals' intelligence parameter is higher than that of low verbals the researcher may end up taking sample cases from the lower range of intelligence of high verbal population; and from the higher range of intelligence of low verbal population. This will defeat random sampling through the two populations, making observations thus obtained untenable for their respective populations. So far as controlling for intelligence at data analysis level is concerned, this involves making observation for intelligence simultaneous with observing high and low verbal *S*s for non-language cognition performance; looking into their difference on intelligence measure; and if it is found statistically significant, partialling out its effect on non-language cognition scores statistically while testing group differences on these scores. This procedure nullifies the confounding effect of intelligence while retaining randomized sampling across the whole range of populations of high and low verbal groups. The present study followed later procedure to eliminate the possible confounding effect of intelligence while looking into the non-language cognitive performances of high and low verbal children of primary grade levels.

Method

Design

The study involved a 2x3 factorial design with 2 levels of verbal ability (i.e. high and low verbal *S*s) being orthogonally combined into three levels of grade dimension (i.e. grades-II, III and V). There were 30 *S*s in each of the six resulting cells. Thus, the total N = 180 in the final sample.

Subject Selection

The sample selection was done in two phases. The initial sample consisted of 150 *S*s drawn randomly from grades-II, III and V. All these *S*s were administered with grade-specific Language Achievement Test Battery (LATB, Sahu, Patnaik and Mishra, 1978, 1979) to assess their level of proficiency in Oriya language. Each LATB was specially developed and standardised for specific grade level. On the basis of the scores obtained on LATB the top 30 *S*s of each grade were labelled as high verbals and bottom 30 as low verbals. The final sample consisted of these high and low verbal *S*s from grades II, III and V.

Tests

Language Achievement Test Battery (LATB)

Three different Language Achievement Test Batteries were used in the present study: one for grade II, one for grade III, and one for grade V.

All these tests aimed to assess *S*s levels of competence in Oriya language. Oriya is the mother tongue of the present sample. The LATB for grade II contained 3 sub-tests: (a) a test of reading, (b) a test of word comprehension, and (c) a test of listening comprehension. The LATBs for grades III and V contained 4 sub-tests each: (a) a test of spelling, (b) a test of word comprehension, (c) a test of listening comprehension, and (d) a test of word fluency. Scores on these sub-tests were summed to get the total score.

Tests of Cognition

Three tests were used to assess *S*s' cognitive performance. They were : picture completion test; block design test; and a test of coding. All these sub-tests were taken from Bhatt's Indian Adoption of WISC Battery (Bhatt, 1973).

Picture Complection Test: This test contained visual pictures of 20 different items. In each of these pictures there is a missing part. The *S*'s task is to identify the missing part in each of these pictures. The test started with quite easy items and gradually increased in difficulty level.

Block Design Test: This test consisted of a series of coloured block design pictures. The *S*'s task is to construct a block using small coloured wooden blocks similar to the one given in the picture. Here also the test strated with easy items and gradually increased in difficulty level.

Test of Coding: This test consisted of a series of a few geometrical symbols. Each symbol is to be marked in a specific way. First, the *S* is instructed as to how to mark each symbol. *S*'s task consists of marking all the figures presented to him in a series within a specific time limit. This was a speed test.

Test of Intelligence

Raven's Coloured Progressive Matrices (RCPM, Raven, 1962) was used as the non-verbal measure of intelligence in the present study. This test consists of a series of increasingly difficult items. Each test item has a bigger picture with a missing part in it. Six smaller pictures are there as alternatives below the bigger picture and one of these alternatives fits exactly into the missing space. The *S* has to identify the alternative that appropriately fills the gap.

Test Administration

All the tests were individually administered to all the *S*s by one of the authors.

High and low verbal *S*s of grade II scored 15.80 and 12.13 (mean values) on RPM, 8.00 and 7.00 on picture completion, 9.00 and 4.60 on block design, and 39.00 and 30.60 on coding. These scores for high and low verbals of grade III were 17.00 and 15.00; 11.00 and 9.00; 13.00 and 10.00; and 42.00 and 35.00 respectively. Parallel scores for high and low verbals of grade V were 26.00 and 18.50; 15.00 and 10.00; 20.17 and 10.00; and 47.00 and 44.00.

A 2x3 analysis of variance was done to see the effect of grade, verbal ability and their interaction on RPM scores. Both the main effects were significant (*'F'* ratios were: 86.73 and 67.26 for grade and verbal ability dimensions with $df = 2/174$ and 1/174 and $p < .01$ in each case); and also the interaction effect ($F = 9.23$, $df = 2/174$, $p < .01$). This means that high and low verbals were significantly different on RPM scores. This finding commanded statistical partialling of its' effect on other measures.

Table 9.1 presentes the summary of analyses of covariance (using RPM as covariate in each case) for picture completion, block design and coding scores. All these analyses of covariance were of 2x3 factorial type.

This Table shows that even after partialling out the effect of intelligence grade, verbal ability and their interaction effects were all, significant in all these cases. Figures 9.1, 9.2 and 9.3 depict the interaction effects in all these cases. Figures 9.1 , 9.2 and 9.3 show that while the gap between high and low verbal *S*s widened over grades in case of picture completion and block design tasks, it gradually narrowed down in case of coding.

Discussion and Conclusion

Table 9.2 shows that high verbal *S*s did bettter than their low verbal counterparts on all the non-verbal measures of cognition even after the intelligence effect was partialled out. This establishes the fact that language skills play important role in cognitive operations. But, the exact nature of its role has not been bourne out by the present study. The study did not aim to specify exactly the nature of the role this ability plays in cognitions. Most likely all these functions i.e. directive, organising, coding, and retrival go together, hence, language proficiency facilitates cognitive performance even for tasks which weigh primarily on non-linguistic skills.

TABLE 9.1: Summary of 2 x 3 analysis of covariance (with RPM as covariate in each case) for picture completion, block design, and coding scores

Sources of	Picture Completion		Block Design		Coding	
Variance	MSV	'*F*' ratio	MSV	'*F*' ratio	MSV	'*F*' ratio
Grade	433.64	104.74**	472.12	9.63**	343.86	6.73**
Verbal ability	1326.82	320.48**	820.95	16.74**	696.10	13.73**
Interaction	113.32	27.37**	206.29	4.21*	283.26	5.55**

** $p < .01$

* $p < .05$

So far as interaction effects are concerned picture completion and block design scores show widening gaps between high and low verbal *S*s over grades; whereas coding scores show a narrowing gap. This is probably due to the fact that both picture completion and block design tests are power-cum-speed tests and coding is almost a speed-only test. When a task involves higher mental functions, as in former two cases, language probably plays increasing regulatory roles. Hence, with increasing grades its differential effect become more and more pronounced. On the other hand, when a task is so easy that it is almost a speed-only task, role of language is less and it still decreases once the basic association is established. Younger children take longer time to establish the figure—mark association, older children establish it quickly. Hence, with increasing grade the gap has reduced.

Two relevant points need to be mentioned here. Hunt, Lunneberg and Lewis (1975) proposed that being high on verbal ability basically means to be high on information processing. They point out that verbal tests indirectly tap a person's current information processing (CIP) ability. By current information processing they refer to the "processes by which people detect stimuli, locate them in time and space, and coordinate them in respect to stored representations.........." It is possible that high verbals, of the present study were better information processors. Besides, the concept of working memory (Baddley and Hitch, 1974; Daneman and Carpenter, 1980) as a processing-cum-storage site showing a strong relation to various language skills (Daneman, Carpenter,1980; Ormrod and Cochran, 1988; Das and Siu, 1989; McDonald, 1992; Just and Carpenter, 1992) proposes another possible explanation for the present

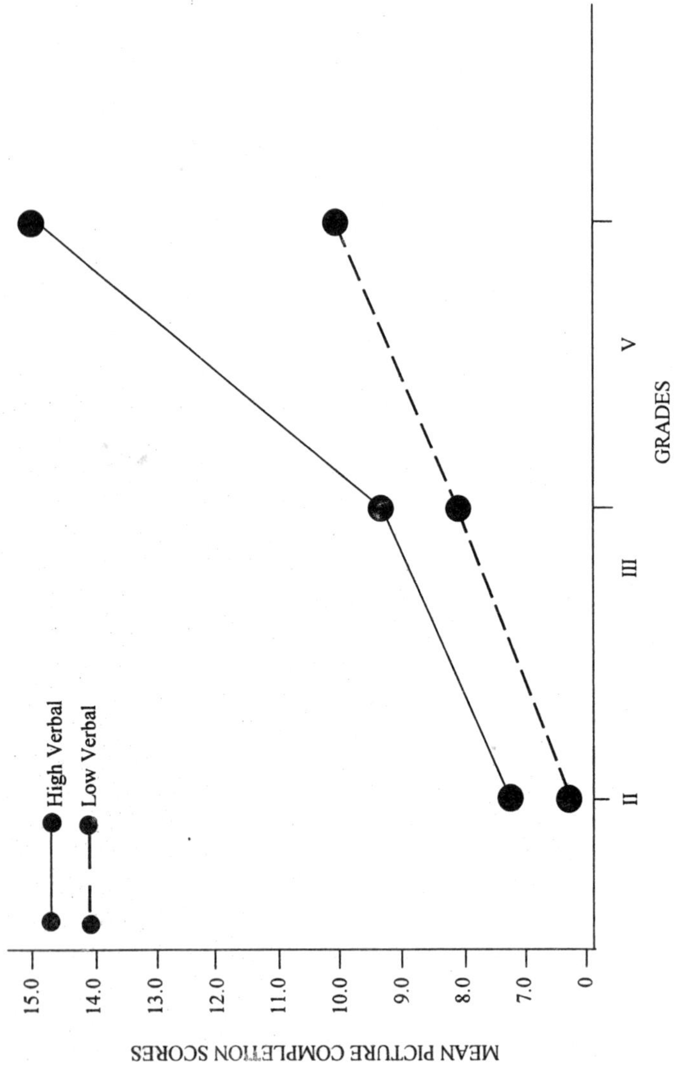

FIG.: 9.1: Figure Showing the performance of high and low verbal *Ss* of grades II, III and V on Picture Completion scores

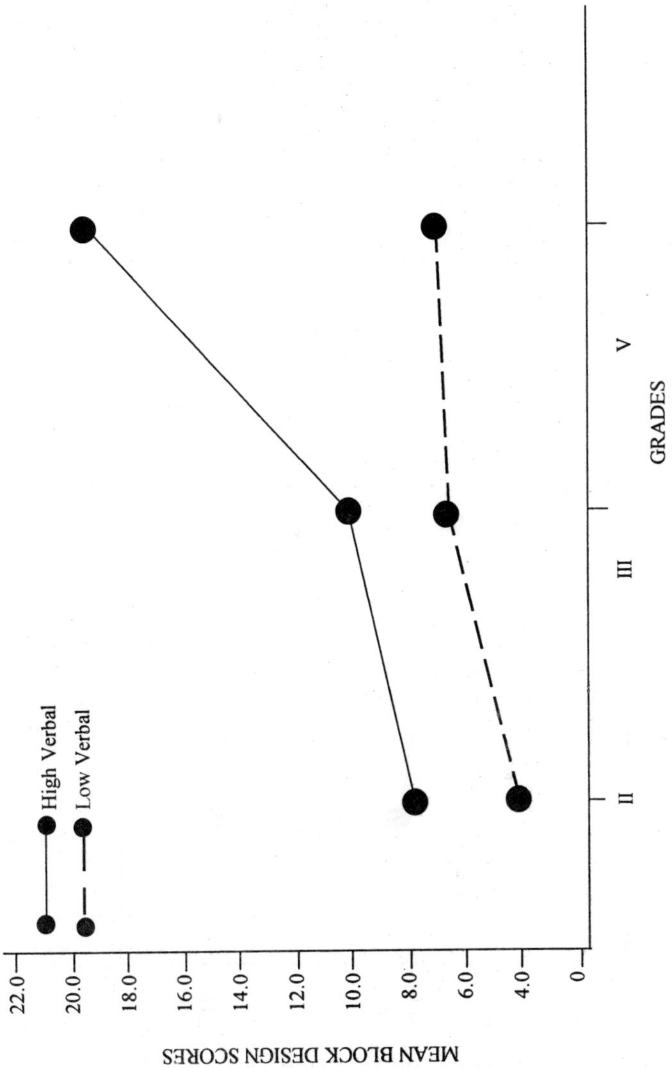

FIG.: 9.2: Figure Showing the performance of high and low verbal *Ss* of grades II, III and V on Block Design Test

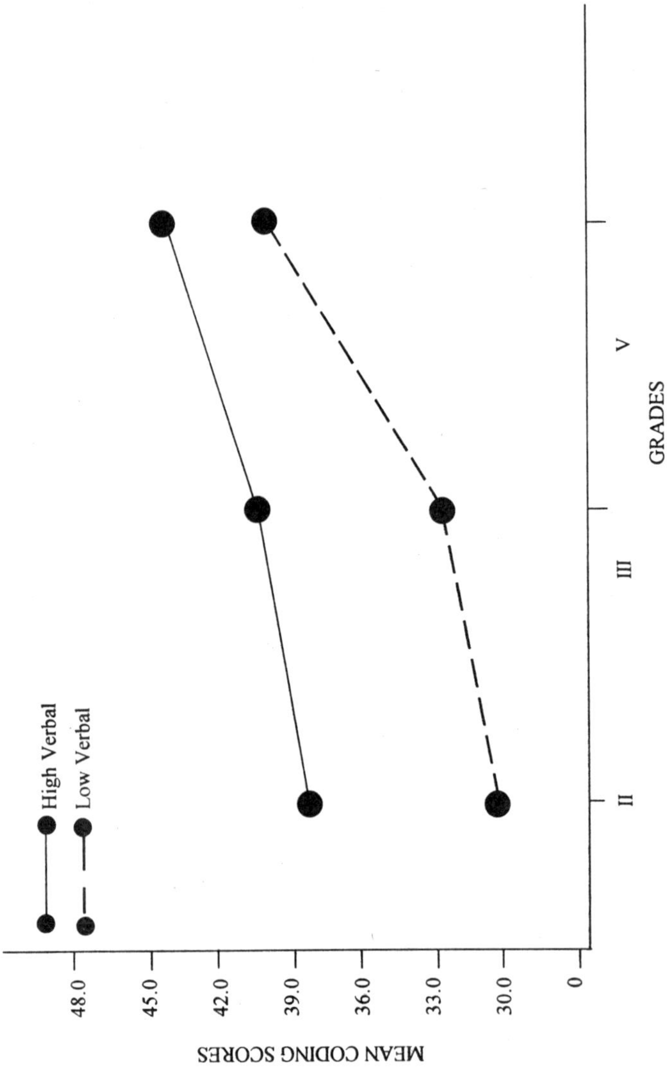

FIG.: 9.3: Figure Showing the performance of high and low verbal *Ss* of grades II, III and V on Coding Test

observation. It is possible that high verbals of the present study had higher working memory capacities. So, could it possible that high verbal Ss possess higher working memory capacities; hence are better information processors, which facilitate their performances across all cognitive tasks ? Future researches may aim to answer this.

Summary

Verbal abilities can be viewed to facilitate cognitive functions by playing directive, organising, coding and retrieval-helping functions. The present study aimed to assess the non-verbal cognitive performances of high and low verbal children of grades-II, III and V. Measures of cognition included picture completion, block design and coding tasks. Confounding effect of intelligence was statistically controlled. Results showed that high verbal children performed better than their low verbal counterparts across all the grade levels; and this discrepancy increased over grade when the task involved higher mental operations. Results have been discussed in the light of task demands vis-a-vis the role played by language factors. The paper suggest that high verbals probably have greater working memory capacity, which results in better current information processing, leading to better performance across all cognitive tasks.

10

RELECTION—IMPULSIVITY AND READING IN ORIYA ORTHOGRAPHY

Orthographic Variations

Writing systems or orthographies vary widely from each other. One way of categorising writing systems is to devide them into logographic, syllabic and alphabetic types (Taylor, 1981; Varsheny, 1985; Reyner and Pollatsek, 1989). This division is based on the principle of extent of correspondance between a character and the level of its representation in language. This representation could be there at the level of a meaningful unit or at the level of a pronounceable unit; or at the level of a part of a speech sound i.e., a phoneme. When in a writing system, as in the case of Chinese, a character stands for a meaningful unit, the writing system is known as a logographic type of orthography. On the other hand, when in a writing system, as in case of Japanese, a character stands for a syllable, it is known as a syllabic orthography. Similarly, when in a writing system, as in case of English, a character stands for a phoneme, it is known as an alphabetic orthography.

Besides, orthographies can also be categorised into phonetic and non-phonetic types. This division is based on the principle of variance or invariance in character-to-phonic conversion. When in an orthography, as in case of English, the character-to-phonic conversion varies depending upon the word context in which it appears, the orthography is known as a non-phonetic orthography (Wanger and Torgesen, 1987). And, when in an orthography, as in case of Hindi, character-to-phonic conversion remains almost invariant across all uses the orthography is known as a phonetic orthography. Thus, orthographies can be broadly classified into six different categories, i.e., logographic, syllabic and alphabetic

---

Co-authors Sujata Mohanty and Sujata Singh

orthographies which are either phonetic or non-phonetic in nature. However, no orthography is absolutely pure an orthography and most are complex mixtures of these characteristics (Reyner and Pollatsek, 1989).

Here, it is pertinent to mention that phonemic and phonetic orthographies may be different from each other (Sgall, 1987). Phonemic orthography is one, where a character stands for a phoneme which is a part of a speech sound and phonetic orthography is one where a character stands for a specific phonetic sound, which remains the same across all uses of the character. A phoneme is not pronounceable by itself. It becomes pronounceable only when it is blended with another phoneme represented by another alphabet. Sound blending in English is an example of this process. On the other hand, in a phonetic orthography a character may be singularly pronounceable by itself; and may not need phonetic blending with another character to be pronounceable as in case of Hindi orthography. Thus, the basic difference between a phonemic and phonetic orthography, from the point of view of print-to-sound conversion is that reading in a phonemic orthography is necessarily sound-blending dependent; where as it may not be so in case of a phonetic orthography.

Orthography and Reading

Orthography variations can have significant implications for reading; especially for oral reading. Oral reading can be broadly viewed as giving phonic sounds for printed matter. This process may or may not involve comprehension or understanding of the text (Danks and Fears, 1979).

So far as the process of giving phonic sounds to prints is concerned, it involves the reading strategy taken by a reader, which in turn, is related to the cognitive demands to be bourne by him. And, reading strategies could be different for different orthographies.

When an orthography is syllablic and phonetic, reader may focus attention on one letter of the word at a time, give its phonic sound; and then may move to the next letter in the same word. In this process he can end up giving the correct phonic conversion of the whole word, without concurrently holding all its letters in working memory. Thus, he can take a micro-approach to reading words. On the other hand, when an orthography is not syllabic (may be alphabetic) and also nonphonetic in nature, a reader can not afford to take such a micro-approach for reading words. He has to scan the whole word, hold its component letters in working memory, make the orthography—specific sound blending, and then give the phonic conversion for the word. In other words, in such a case, (as in case of English) the reader has to take a macro - approach for reading words.

The possibilities of micro-and macro-reading approaches, in their turn, can have implications for the cognitive load they put on the reader. It can be expected that a micro-reading approach will make less demand on the working memory capacity of the reader than a macro-approach, since, in the former case he does not have to hold all the information content of a word at a time; nor has to make necessary sound-blending with these information before giving a phonic conversion for it. But, these processes are necessary prerequisites before a correct response is elicitated in the latter case.

However, a possible cognitive fall out can be expected out of these two reading strategies: a micro-reading approach may produce more word-callers than a macro-reading approach. Since in the former case the reader converts each character into a sound, he may end up with little understanding of the word, especially if he is a beginning reader. On the other hand, in case of a micro-reader since he holds and manipulates with all the information content of a word, it is likely that he would gain insight and then hit at its meaning better.

Thus, orthographic variations may lead to different reading strategies, may make different cognitive (working memory, to be specific) demands, and may lead to differential insights into word-meaning.

Reflection and Impulsivity

Cognitive style refers to one's habitual mode of attacking a cognitive task. Kogan (1971) points out that it may be defined as individual variations in modes of preceiving, remembering and thinking, or as distinctive ways of apprehending, storing, transforming, and utilising information. As many as nineteen such styles have been suggested as yet. Reflection-impulsivity are two of them suggested by Kagan, Rosman, Day, Albert and Phillips (1964). Reflection-impulsivity describes the tendency to reflect on the validity of problem solving under a very special condition, namely, when several possible alternatives are available and there is some uncertainty over which one is the most appropriate (Messer, 1976). Kagan and his associates discovered that in problem solving situations with high response uncertainty, children who proceed by slow deliberation, make fewer errors, while others who respond in a quick, hasty, impulsive fashion, make many errors. Both Kagan (1971); and Kagan and Kogan (1970) from their extensive reviews of literature on individual variations in cognitive processes, conclude that this disposition toward either a reflective or impulsive style has been found to be reliable and stable over time and generalizes to a variety of cognitive tasks.

The instrument most often used to measure reflection-impulsivity is the Matching Familiar Figures Tests (MFFT; Kagan *et al.*, 1964). Operationally, reflectivity is defined as a long response latency with few errors and impulsivity as a short response latency with frequent errors. The MFFT test has been found to be a reliable and valid measure (Messer, 1976).

Researchers have tried to look into the scanning strategies of reflective and impulsive children. It has been observed that reflectives examined the minute details of all the possible alternatives before choosing one and also spent longer time in comparing pairs or stimuli that included the standard and an alternative, as well as scanned all other pairs in minute details. They have been found to be thorough in comparing pairs before making a choice. By contrast, the viewing behaviour of impulsives have been found to be less systematic and more global. They do not scan the field for distinctive feature as systematically as reflectives do. Thus studies show that scanning strategies of reflective and impulsive subjects differ (Messer,1976).

Reflection—Impulsivity and Reading Strategy: Observations in English Orthography

Researches have tried to relate this facet of cognitive style to the reading performance of subjects. Since impulsive and reflective subjects basically differ in their scanning strategies and attention to details, and reading starts with visual input, researchers expected that this would lead to differential competence in reading performance. Walters and Doan (1962), Kagan (1965), Abikoff (1979), and Sousley and Gargiulo (1981) studies point to the fact that impulsive subjects show reading retardation. Impulsives have been found to make more recognition errors in reading English words presented singularly or in a prose selection. Though researchers have explained in different ways the relationship between impulsivity and reading errors yet it remains a fact that in the context of English orthography impulsivity is related to reading incompetence.

Oriya Orthography; its Unique Features and Implications for Reading

Oriya is one of the officially recognised languages of India. It belongs to the group of Indo-Aryan languages. Its script is a variation of Brahmi script (Pattanayak, 1969). It has 47 letters out of which 12 are vowels and 35 are consonants. The typical way of writing Oriya consists of making two different circles, a smaller one and a bigger one, on the top of it. Distinguishing features are made in either or both of these circles and make up a letter. Apart from 47 letters, vowels can be symbolically added to different consonants. When a vowel is symbolically appended to a consonant it is called a *matra.* Addition of a *matra* slightly changes the phonic sound of the consonant. Addition of *matras* to different consonants provide for a wide variety of spelling possibilities with meaning differences. Besides, consonants can also be represented symbolically and be appended to other consonants. When this is done it is called a *phala.* Addition of a *phala* to a consonant makes a compound consonant or a conjunct character. *Matras* and *phalas* are appended to consonants in the form of superscripts, side-scripts, or subscripts.

In addition, Oriya writing system provides for combination of different consonants which are called *yuktakshyaras* (Praharaj, 1936; Padhi, 1971). These *yuktakshyaras* can be viewed as cluster graphemes.

Apart from *matras, phalas* and *yuktakshyaras* there are a few characters in Oriya orthography which involve doubling of a single consonant. Such a character is written by putting the original consonant first and making a symbolic representation of the same consonant below it. Such doubled characters retain the original phonic representation of the consonant with a greater emphasis on it.

Oriya writing system can be viewed as an alphabatic syllabic type of phonetic writing system. It is alphabatic syllabic in the sense that each consonant in conjunction with a vowel makes a syllabic. It is phonetic in the sense that the grapheme-to-phoneme correspondence is almost invariant across all uses of the grapheme. Each letter has letter name and this letter name is the phonetic mapping of the concerned grapheme. This phonetic mapping of the grapheme is retained irrespective of the grapheme's use in different word contexts. Oriya writing system, thus, has a built-in phonetic pattern.

Most of the researches in the field of psychology of reading till date have been done in the context of English orthography. English and Oriya orthographies differ from each other on significant points and these differences can be expected to have significant implications for reading strategies and processes.

English can be viewed to be an alphabetic and non-phonetic orthography. Each character of English orthography is an alphabet in the sense that it stands for a phoneme, which is a part of a speech sound. A phoneme is not singularly pronounceable, hence, needs to be blended with another phoneme to make it pronounceable. Sound-blending techniques as per orthography-specific rules form a necessary prerequisite for mastery over reading skill. Moreover, it is a non-phonetic orthography in the sense that the grapheme-to-phoneme correspondence, far from being invariant, is dependent upon the word context in which a particular grapheme appears. Thus English is an alphabetic and non-phonetic writing system where sound blending techniques play important role in reading processes.

English being an alphabetic, non-phonetic writing system demanding sound blending skills, can be visualized to be making greater cognitive demands on its reader. To be specific, probably it demands a larger working memory capacity. Because, its reader has to take a macro-reading strategy hence has to hold all the bits of information contained in a word in concurrent memory and make sound blending manipulations before giving a correct reading of the word.

On the other hand, since Oriya is a syllabic and phonetic writing system a micro level reading strategy would be sufficient to give a correct reading of a word. That is, the reader may focus his attention on one letter of the word, give its phonic conversion, and then may shift to the next letter contained in the same word. In this process he can give the correct phonic conversion of the whole word without scanning the whole word at a time and holding all its information in the concurrent memory. Besides, sound blending between the characters is not necessary. This, in turn, may mean a lesser demand on the working memory capacity of the reader.

Reflection-Impulsivity and Reading in Oriya Orthography

Oral Reading: Reading could be broadly defined as the process of getting the meaning from a text. It could be visualised to be consisting of two broad facets: oral reading and reading comprehension. Oral reading basically consists of reading aloud the contents of a print. Thus this facet of reading is more concerned with graphic-to-phonic conversion than with comprehension of the text. But when this conversion takes place the reder may hit at the meaning of the text. Danks and Fears (1979) propose that oral reading may or may not involve comprehension. Reading comprehension, on the other hand, basically is concerned with arriving at the meaning of the text. Here, the reader may or may not read the text loudly, but his main target is to arrive at the meaning. So, reading comprehension may involve loud reading or it may involve silent reading of the text.

Present authors did a study which aimed to look into the oral reading proficiencies of reflective and impulsive groups of children reading in Oriya orthography. Possible confounding effect of intelligence was planned to be partialled out. This study also proposed to look into the reading strategy differences, if any, of these children. Besides, the study proposed to assess possible developmental changes in this context.

Sample cases for the study were drawn from two grade levels, that is, grades III and V. The initial sample consisted of 80 children drawn from each grade. All these children were administered with Matching Familiar Figures Test (MFFT, Kagan *et al.,* 1964). Observations of response latency scores and error scores of subjects (*Ss*) revealed that *Ss* who normally had high response latency had low error scores, and *Ss* who had low response latencies had high error scores. This trend was present in both the grade levels. Hence on the basis of latency and error scores *Ss* were finally selected for reflective and impulsive groups at both grade levels. At grade III level the reflective group had a mean ($\overline{X}$) latency score of 641.60 seconds (SD = 50.11) and a mean error score of 7.1 (SD = 3.55). The impulsives at this grade had the mean latency score of 213.00 seconds (SD =23.92) and a mean error score of 30.66 (SD = 7.39). In case of grade V *Ss* the reflective group had a mean response latency score of 479.30 seconds (SD = 167.06) and a mean error score of 3.86 (SD =3.69). The impulsive group of this grade had a mean time score, of 172.43 seconds (SD =77.79) and a mean error score of 25.56 (SD = 8.07). N was 30 in each case. Thus the final sample for the study consisted of impulsive and reflective *Ss* from grades III and V with N = 30 in each case. So, the final sample consisted of 120 *Ss*.

All these *Ss* were administered with grade-appropriate oral reading tasks (Sahu and Patnaik, 1987) and Raven's Coloured progressive Matrices (Raven, 1962). Oral Reading Tasks consisted of sentences and the subjects were required to read them aloud. As the *Ss* read the sentences the experimenter recorded the exact response of the *S* which were then scored for number of words read correctly, number of words read incorrectly (i.e. miscues), number of words added during reading, number of words omitted during reading, and complete failures. Besides, the time taken to complete the reading task was being recorded.

Reflective and impulsive *Ss* of grade III had mean ($\overline{X}$) age of 90.43 and 89.70 (in months) respectively. Their $\overline{X}$ RCPM scores were

24.23 and 20.86. Mean correct (CR) and incorrect (IR) reading scores were 151.27 and 145.33; and 4.57 and 8.03. Similarly, reflective and impulsive *S*s of grade V had $\bar{X}$ age scores of 122.33 and 122.83 (in months). RCPM scores were 28.97 and 26.97 respectively. Mean CRs were 417.90 and 396.60; and IRs were 12.17 and 29.33.

In order to see if the RCPM differences were significant *'t'* tests were performed. The *'t'* ratio for grade III was 3.22 and for grade V it was 6.61. Both these *'t'* ratios were signifiicant at .01 level. This observation necessitated statistical partialling of the effect of RCPM variance on reading performance difference during further analyses. Hence during further analyses this effect was statistically partialled out through the application of analyses of covariance (Winer, 1971). Table 10.1 presents the results of these analyses of covariance for grades III and V.

Table 10.1 shows that reflective *S*s performed significantly better than impulsive *S*s on measures of oral reading performance even after the intelligence effect was partialled out. This was true at both grade levels. This observation means that better performance of reflective *S*s on oral reading tasks is not accountable by intelligence differences.

Miscue Analyses

Wrong readings are known as miscues. Miscue, analysis has been used as a technique to reveal the reading strategy of a reader (Goodman, 1969; Potter, 1980; Potter, 1981; Francis, 1984). In the present study miscues were analysed to see the extent of use of orthographic and context cues (sementic and syntactic) during reading. Reflectives were slightly higher on these indices. But these differences were not statistically significant.

Discussion

Results of this study show that reflective *S*s were better oral readers than impulsive *S*s. As has already been pointed out, reflective *S*s happen to be better scanners of the stimuli presented. They minutely scan each alternative before making a choice; and also compare between alternatives for their appropriateness under a given circumstance before finally selecting an alternative for the problem situation. On the other hand impulsive *S*s scan alternatives globally without looking into their minute details and without looking into the minute differences between

TABLE 10.1: Summeries of analyses of covariance for correct and incorrect reading responses of Grades-III and V *Ss*. RCPM was taken to be the covariate in all cases

Sources of Variance	*df*	Grade- III				Grade- V			
		CR		IR		CR		IR	
		MSV	*F*	MSV	*F*	MSV	*F*	MSV	*F*
Error	57	7.50	—	2.57	—	25911.77	—	64.57	—
Treatments	1	197.14	26.29**	111.44	43.36**	1464513.30	56.52**	3742.09	57.95**

** $p < .01$

alternatives and checking for their appropriateness under a given situation. It is probably such differences in viewing the reflective *S*s end up in giving more correct oral reading responses for the same reading text than comparable impulsives. In case of a text reading situation the visual inputs come from the print and a reader has to carefully view the word for its distinctive letter contents before giving possible reading responses to it, being guided by expectancy patterns. Expectancies in turn, are set by discriminant letter contents of words. It is natural that a careful viewing and scanning would help giving higher correct reading scores.

Reading Comprehension

Reading comprehension refers to the process of getting at the meaning of a text. Some authors view that reading is incomplete without comprehension.

So far as the measures of comprehension are concerned passage comprehension tasks and cloze tasks have been widely used. In case of a passage comprehension task *S* is presented with a written passage and after he goes through it he is required to answer several questions relating to the passage. These questions could be of literal comprehension type or inferential comprehension type. A literal comprehension question tries to elicit exact information contained in the passage. Such a question mainly weighs on the memory of the reader. An inferential comprehension question, on the other hand, tries to assess the inference making ability of the reader on the basis of the bits of information contained in the text. Such a question weighs on the inferencing ability of the reader. On the other hand, a cloze task consists of a paragraph with some words deleted from it. The subject is asked to go through this paragraph and then to suggest words for places of deletions. Subject's responses are then analysed for their correctness. Comprehension takes place taking cues from the existing contents of the paragraph. A reader who comprehends the paragraph despite the delections is able to provide appropriate words for places of delections.

Present authors did a study to look into the reading comprehension processes of reflective and impulsive *S*s reading in Oriya orthography. Confounding effect of intelligence was planned to be partialled out. The sample was drawn from grade-V ensuring fluent oral reading, so that reading comprehension tasks could be administered on them. The initial sample consisted of 90 *S*s from grade-V drawn from a primary school. All these children were administered with MFFT (Kagan *et al.,* 1964) test. *Ss* for refletive and impulsive groups were finally selected on the basis of response latency scores and error scores. The reflective group consisted of 30 *Ss* with a mean latency score of 600.34 seconds (SD = 57.76) and a mean error score of 13.13 (SD = 6.56). The impulsive group consisted of 30 *Ss* with a mean latency score of 222.98 seconds (SD = 56.54) and a mean error score of 25.60 (SD = 6.45). The mean differences on latency and error scores were significant (*'t'* ratios were 12.34 and 7.34, both with $p < .01$). Mean age of reflective group was 116.43 months (SD = 5.83) and the same for impulsive group was 117.57 months (SD = 5.77). Age difference was not statistically significant (*'t'* = 0.74, $p > .05$).

The final sample of 60 *Ss* was administered with grade appropriate passage comprehension task, cloze task and Raven's Coloured Progressive Matrices (RCPM). In case of the passage comprehension task the subject was required to answer a set of comprehension questions. 'Answer to these questions were scored for their correctness and failure. In case of cloze task *Ss*' responses were scored for their correctness and incorrectness; and if incorrect for their acceptability in the passage context. Responses which exactly tallied with the deleted word were taken as correct responses; and responses which did not tally with exact words deleted were taken as incorrect responses. Some of the responses which were incorrect were found to be acceptable in the given passage context. Such responses were taken as incorrect but acceptable responses. The rest of the incorrect responses were categoried as incorrect and unacceptable responses.

The mean ($\overline{X}$) passage comprehension scores of reflective and impulsive *Ss* were : 9.50 and 7.80 (for correct responses), 10.27 and 11.50 (for incorrect responses), 0.23 and 0.70 (for failures). For cloze performance these $\overline{X}$ values were 12.14 and 12.27 (for correct responses), 20.87 and 20.73 (for incorrect responses). Incorrect acceptable responses were 10.03 and 8.27; incorrect unacceptable responses were 10.83 and 12.47 for reflective and impulsive groups respectively.

The reflectives had a mean RCPM value of 23.06 and impulsives 18.00. In order to see if reflective and impulsive *Ss* differed significantly on RCPM scores a *'t'* test was done. The *'t'* ratio was 2.83 with $p < 0.01$. Hence in order to see the significance of difference between reflective and impulsive *Ss* on measures of comprehension, analyses of covariance were done, taking RCPM as the covariate. Analyses of covariance for correct passage comprehension score yielded an F ratio of 5.26 which was significant at .05 level. All other covariance results were insignificant.

Discussion

Reading comprehension involves going deeper into the matters of the text. It not only involves appropriate scanning and viewing strategies, it also involves inferencing processes and deep level linguistic processing. Results of the present study show that compared to impulsives reflectives did better on different measures of comprehension and it was significant for correct passage comprehension scores.

General Discussion and Conclusion

Two studies in the context of Oriya writing system were carried out aiming to look into two different facets of reading processes. Reflective and impulsive *S*s were employed. Study looking into oral reading processes observed that reflective *S*s were significantly better oral readers. This difference existed even after RCPM effect was partialled out.

Study looking into reading comprehension processes observed that reflective *S*s were better performers on measures of comprehension. This trend was significant for correct passage comprehension scores.

Studies in the context of English orthography point to the fact that reflective *S*s are better at reading performances. Present studies probed into the reading performances in the context of Oriya orthography. Present findings coroborate observations made in the context of English orthography. This probably implies that despite orthographic differences reflective and impulsive readers take similar reading strategies while attacking reading task.

Summary

Writing systems or orthographies vary widely from each other; and orthographic variations have significant bearing on reading competence. This is probably because different orthographies make different cognitive and reading strategy demands on its reader. Reading researches across different orthographies employing reflective and impulsive *S*s are necessary to locate exactly the impact of these two cognitive approaches on reading processes.

Orthographies are broadly divided into logographic, syllabic and alphabatic orthographies; and also into phonetic and non-phonetic orthographies. Studies relating reflection-impulsive cognitive styles to reading processes have mostly been done in the context of English orthography, which is an alphabetic and non-phonetic orthography. Researches in the context of logographic, syllabic, and phonetic orthographies are rather few.

Oriya orthography is an alphabatic syllabic phonetic orthography. Reading research in the context of Oriya orthography using reflective and impulsive children across two primary grades looked into their oral reading competence and strategies. Reflectives were found to be more competent oral readers than the comparable impulsives; and this difference was sustained even after the effect of intelligence was partialled out. Miscue analysis revealed that reflective *S*s were better users of orthographic and context cues during reading though this difference was not significant. Study looking into the reading comprehension of reflective and impulsive *S*s reading in Oriya orthography showed that here also, on some measures reflective *S*s performed significantly better than impulsive *S*s and this difference was sustained even after intelligence effect was partialled out. Better oral reading and reading comprehension performance of reflective children has been attributed to an approproiate scanning strategy and better use of semantic, syntactic, and orthographic cues during reading.

EPILOGUE

Other Thoughts

Studies reported in this monograph are confined to primary grade level children only. Primary grade level presents a stage when reading skills are acquired and mastered. Competence or incompetence; successes and failures at this level implicate at future reading competence or failure. Looking into such successes or failures and their reasons through miscue analysis; or through correlating them with underlying cognitive processes would help a researcher planning corrective measures. Hence exploratory studies, as this monograph reports, were conducted using primary grade level children.

But, reading processes and strategies at later stage in life may not present a simple quantitative growth from this stage, it may show a completely different qualitative growth. Hence, looking into reading processes beyoned the primary grade level are pertinent in locating the developmental changes that take place; and also in planning corrective procedures in case reading failures occur.

Besides, studies in the field of reading difficulty have not been reported here. No study has been done to look if reading disabled children exist among Oriya readers. If they exist, no attempt has been made to look at the rate of their incidence. So also, no study has been undertaken attempting corrective measures for children with reading difficulty/disability. Such stuides are needed in order to make reading research findings practically applicable.

However, it is viewed that reading difficulties or incompetence may exist among Oriya reading children with normal intelligence, who have speech, hearing or visual handicap. But, children without any handicap and taking normal reading skill instructions may only differ from each other in regard to their reading competence. This difference may range from the point of being a very good reader to the point of being a very poor reader. Individual differences within the normal probability range can exist for average readers of Oriya orthography. But readers of Oriya orthography are unlikely to come up with reading disability; which is defined as a lag in reading performance by two grades. Such extreme cases are unlikely to exist among average population. This contention is based on the reasoning that Oriya is an alphabatic-syllabic-phonetic orthography. Hence, factors like sound blending skills which is one of the causes of reading failure would not play a role in determining reading success of Oriya readers. Research reports in the context of English orthography point to the fact that failure at sound blending skills some times lie at the core of reading problems. This, in turn, is preceded by a poor phonological awareness which shows that a child who has problems in identifying the phonological mapping of a letter in different word contexts, is unable to blend phonemes of letters contained in a word into a meaningful word format. Besides, reading disabled children reading English orthography show poor phonemic segmentation ability. They fail to say how many phonemes are contained in the sound of a word. They also fail to say if a given phoneme is deleted from the sound of a word what other phonemes would still be there. Hence, phonemic segmentation and knowledge about blending of phonemes make up a significant determiner of a child's success or failure at reading English orthography.

Such situations occur because English is an alphabetic (phonemic) and non-phonetic orthography, where not only the phonetic sounds of characters vary, there are also orthography-specific rules for the sound blending of these phonemes. Probably for this nature of the orthography, there is an extra load on the beginning reader to acquire and master these information and skills, and failures at these lead to reading problems.

Oriya orthography being syllabic and phonetic does not need much of sound blending skills for a successful reading. Moreover, the syllabic nature of the orthography makes it easy for a beginner to segment letter sounds contained in a word i.e., phonemic segmentation is easy. The phonetic nature of the orthography does not demand an orthography-specific rule to blend the sound of individual letters contained in a word into a meaningful format. That is, sound blending skills are almost not demanded. It is visualised that with these advantages an average beginner with average reading skill instructions and provisions would not face a situation where he lags into the realm of reading disability, though at the most, he may show a lower skill level.

So far as reading skill instruction procedures are concerned in the context of English orthography it is a matter of debate if phonic instructions are better than look-and-say method of teaching reading. Phonic instruction procedure teaches the basic phonic conversions of letters. It is expected that after a child learns the phonic sounds of letters he will be in a position to know how these sounds are to be blended to make meaningful words. Hence reading skill would be acquired. On the other hand, look-and-say method of teaching reading takes a wholistic approach and teaches a child what the whole word is, while presenting the written version of the same word. Here, it is expected that after learning the names for a few words the child will automatically develop phoneme segmentation skills and sound blending skills. These in turn, will lead to the acquisition of reading skill. It is a matter of controversy as to which method is a better method to teach reading, also, if a combination of these two methods would prove to be most fruitful.

Such a controversy does not arise in the context of teaching reading in Oriya orthography. While learning individual letters the child learns the letter names, hence, masters the phonic sound. Sound blending for reading words are mostly not needed. Thus, teaching learning and writing alphabets automatically involves phonic training. This is supplemented with look-and-say training where the child is made to respond to whole words. Teaching reading in Oriya thus involves a combination of phonic training and look-and-say approaches. Because of the very nature of the orthography, considerations as to if phonic training would help or hamper do not come up.

However, all these are guesses based on reasonings. Future researches would answer if these guesses are correct.

BIBLIOGRAPHY

Abikoss, H. (1979). Cognitive training intervention in children: Review of a new approach. *Journal of Learning Disabilities,* 12, 123-135.

Ashman, A. (1978). The Relationship between planning and simultaneous and successive synthesis. Unpublished Ph. D. dissertation, Department of Educational Psychology, University of Alberta, Edmonton, Canada.

Baddley, A.D., and Hitch, G. (1974). Working Memory. In G.H. Bower (ed.), *The Psychology of Learning and Motivation.* New York: Academic Press.

Baddley, A.D., Thompson, N., and Buchanan, M. (1975). Word length and the structure of short-term memory. *Journal of Verbal Learning and Verbal Behaviour, 14,* 575-589.

Baddley, A.D. and Hitch, G. (1974). Working Memory. In G.H. Bower (Ed.). *The Psychology of Learning and Motivation, Vol. 8,* New York: Academic Press.

Beardsley, G. (1982). Context cues in early reading. *Journal of Research in Reading, 5,* 101-112.

Besner, D. (1990). Orthographies and their phonologies: A hypothesis. *Bulletin of the Phychonomic Society, 28,* 395-396.

Bhatt, M.C. (1973). *Gujarati Adaptation of Wechsler Intelligence Scale for Children.* Ahmedabad: Dr. M.C. Bhatt.

Broota, K.D. (1989). *Experimental Design in Behavioural Research.* New Delhi, India: Wiley Eastern Ltd.

Burke, E. (1977). A developmental study of children's reading strategies. *Educational Studies, 3,* 137-143.

Case, R., Kurland, D.M., & Goldberg, J. (1982). Operational efficiency of short-term memory span. *Journal of Experimental Psychology, 33,* 386-404.

Cowan, N. (1988). Evolving Conceptions of memory storage, selective attention, and their mutual contraints within the human information-processing system, *Psychological Bulletin, 104,* 163-191.

Cummins, J. & Das, J.P. (1977). Cognitive processing and reading sifficulties: A framework for research, *Alberta Journal of Educational Research, 23,* 245-256.

Danks, J.H., and Fears, R. (1979). Oral reading: Does it reflect decoding or comprehension ? In L.B. Resnick, and P.A. Weaver, (Eds.), *Theory and Practice of Early Reading, Vol. III,* New Jersy : LEA.

Daneman, M., and Carpenter, P.A. (1980). Individual difference in working memory and reading. *Journal of Verbal Learning and Verbal Behaviour, 19,* 450-466.

Daneman, M., and Green, I. (1986). Individual differences in comprehending and producing words in context. *Journal of Memory and Language, 25,* 1-18.

Das, J.P.(1980). Planning: Theoretical considerations and empirical evidence. *Psychological Research, 41,* 141-151.

Das,J.P., Kirby, J. & Jarman, R. F. (1975). Simultaneous and successive synthesis: An alternative model for cognitive abilities, *Psychological Bulletin, 82,* 87-103.

Das, J.P., Kirby, J.R., and Jarman, R. F. (1979). *Simultaneous and Successive Cognitive Processes,* New York: Academic Press.

Das, J.P. & Jarman, R.F. (1981). Coding and planning process. In M.P. Friedman, J.P. Das & N.O'Connor (Ed.). Intelligence and Learning, *NATO Conference Series, Series-III,* New York : Plenum Press.

Das, J.P. and Mensinck, D. (1989). K-ABC Simultaneous sequential scales and prediction of achievement in reading and mathematics. *Journal of Psychoeducational Assessment,* 7(2), 103-111.

Das, J.P., and Siu, I. (1989). Good and poor readers' word naming time, memory span and story recall; *Journal of Experimental Education, 57,* 101-114.

Das, J.P., Naglieri, J.A., and Kirby, J.R. (1994). *Assessment of cognitive Processes: The PASS Theory of Intelligence,* Massachuetts: Allyn & Bacon.

Ehri, L.C. (1980). The development of orthographic images. In U. Frith (Ed.) *Cognitive Processes in Spelling.* Academic Press: London.

Ellis, N. (1990). Reading, phonological skills and short-term memory: interactive tributaries of development. *Journal of Research in Reading, 13,* 107-122.

Engle, R.W., Nations, J.K., and Cantor, J. (1990). Is ''Working memory capacity just another name for word knowledge capacity'' ? *Journal of Educational Psychology, 82,* 799-804.

Frith, U. (1979). Reading by eye and writing by ear. In P.A. Kolers M.E. Wrolstad; and H. Bouma (Edts.), *Processing of Visible Language, Vol.I,* New York: Plenum Press.

Francis, H. (1982). *Learning to Read: Literate Behaviour and Orthographic Knowledge.* London: George Allen and Unwin.

Francis, H. (1984). Children's knowledge of orthography in learning to Read. *British Journal of Educational Psychology, 54* (1), 8-23.

Goodman, K.S. (1969). Analysis of oral reading miscues: Applied psycholinguistics. *Reading Research Quarterly, 5,* 9-30.

Goodman, K.S. and Goodman, Y. M. (1979). Learning to read is natural. In L.B. Resnick and P. Weaver (Eds.), *Theory and Practice of Early Reading, Vol. I,* New Jersy: LEA Publishers.

Goodman, K.S. (1980). Reading: A Psycholinguistic Guessing Game. In H. Singer & B. Ruddell (Ed.). *Theoretical Models and Processes of Reading,* New York: D.E. International Reading Association.

Graham, F.K., & Kendall, B.S.(1960). Memory for designs test : Revised general manual, *Perceptual and Motor, Skills, 11,* 147-188.

Guttenteg, R.E. (1982). A Comment on "Phonological recoding and reading". *Psychological Bulletin, 91,* 366-368.

Hockett, C.F. (1970). *A Course on Modern Linguistics.* New Delhi: Oxford and IBH Publishing Co.

Hunt, E., Lunneberg, C., and Lewis, J. (1975). What does It mean to be high verbal? *Cognitive Psychology, 7,* 194-227.

Hynd, G.W., and Semrud-Clickman, M. (1989). Dyslexia and Brain morphology. *Psychological Bulletin, 106,* 447-482.

Ilg, F.L. & Ames, L.B. (1964). *School readiness: Behaviour Tests used at the Gesell Institute.* New York: Harper & Row.

Jorm, A.F.(1983). Specific reading retardation and working memory: A Review. *British Journal of Psychology,* 74, 311-342.

Juola, J.F.; Schadler, M.; Chabot, R.; Mc Caughey, M.; & Wait, J. (1979). What do children learn when they learn to read ? In L.B. Resnick & P.A. Weaver (Eds.) *Theory and Practice of Early Reading (Vol.II).* Lowrance Erlbaum Associates: Hillsdale, N.J.

Just, M.A., and Carpenter, P.A. (1992). A capacity theory of comprehension: Individual differences in working memory. *Psychological Review, 99,* 122-149.

Kagan, J. (1965). Individual differences in the resolution of response uncertainty, *Journal of Personality and Social Psychology, 2,* 154-160.

Kagan, J., Rosman, S.L., Day, D., Albert, J., & Phillips, R. (1964). Information processing in the child: Significance of analytic and reflective attitudes. *Psychological Monograph, 78* (1, whole No. 575).

Kagan, J., and Kogan, N. (1970). Individual variation in cognitive processes. In P.H. Hussen (Edt.) Charmichaels. *Manual of Child Psychology* (3rd ed.), New York : Willey.

Kogan, N. (1971). Educational implications of cognitive styles. In G. Lesser (Ed.), *Psychology and Educational Practice;* Glenview, 111, Scoff, Foresman.

Kershner, J.R. (1977). Cerebral dominance in disabled readers, good readers, and gifted children: Search for a valid model. *Child Development, 48,* 61-67.

Kimura, Y. (1984). Concurrent vocal interference: Its effect on Kana and Kanji. *Quarterly Journal of Experimental Psychology, 36A,* 117-132.

Kirby, J.R. & Das, J.P. (1977). Reading achievement, IQ, and simultaneous sucessive processing. *Journal of Educational Psychology, 69,* 564-570.

Kirk, S.A., Mc Carthy, J.J., and Kirk, D. (1968). *Illinois Test of Psycholinguistic Abilities.* Urbana: University of Illinois Press.

Kohlberg, L., Yaeger, J., and Hjertholm. (1968). Private Speech: Four studies and a review of theories, *Child Development, 39,* 691-736.

Laberge, D., and Samuel, S.J. (1974). Toward a theory of automatic information processing in reading. *Cognitive Psychology, 6,* 223-232.

Leong, C.K. (1980). Cognitive patterns of 'retarded' and below average readers. *Contemporary Educational Psychology, 5,* 101-117.

Leong, C.K., (1981). Cognitive strategies in relation to reading disability In M.P. Friedman, J.P. Das & N.O'Connor (Ed.) Intelligence and Learning. *NATO Conference Series, Series-III*, New York: Plenum Press.

Liberman, I.Y. & Shankweiler, D. (1979). Speech, the alphabet and teaching to read. In L.B. Resnick & P.A. Weaver (Eds.) *Theory and Practice of Early Reading* Vol. II., New Jersy: LEA Publishers.

Luria, A.R. (1966a). *Higher Cortical Functions in Man,* New York: Basic Books.

Luria, A. (1966b). *Human Brain and Psychological Processes.* New York: Harper and Row.

Luria, A.R. (1970). The functional organisation of the brain, *Scientific American, 222,* 66-78.

Massaro, D.W.; and Hestand, J. (1983). Developmental relations between reading ability and knowledge of Orthographic structure. *Contemporary Educational Psychology, 8,* 174-180.

Mc Cusker, L.M., Hillinger, M.L., and Bias, R.G. (1981). Phonological recoding and reading. *Psychological Bulletin, 89,* 217-245.

Mc Donald, M.C. (1992). Working memory constraints on the processing of syntactic ambiguity; *Congnitive Psychology, 24,* 56-98.

Mc Leod, R.W. (1978). An exploratory study of reference and cognitive synthesis in reading comprehension with selected grade 4 readers. Unpublished Ph. D. thesis, Department of Elementary Education, University of Alberta, Cannada.

Messer, S.B. (1976) Reflection impulsivity: A review; *Psychological Bulletin, 83,* 1026-1053.

Mensick, S. (1976). Personality consistencies in cognition and creativity. In S. Messick (Ed.). *Individuality in Learning.* San Francisco : Josey-Base.

Mishra, S. (1987). Developmental changes in oral reading strategies, Unpublished dissertation, Department of Psychology, Utkal University, Orissa, India.

Moore, M.J., Kagan, J., Sahl. M. and Grant, S. (1982). Cognitive profiles in reading disability. *Genetic Psychology Monograph, 105,* 41-93.

Murrary, L.A., and Maliphant, R. (1982). Developmental aspects of the use of linguistic and graphemic information during reading. *British Journal of Educationl Psychology, 57,* 155-169.

Naglieri, J.A., Kaufman, A.S., Kaufman, N.L. & Kamphaus, R.W. (1981). Cross-validation of Das simultaneous and successive processes with novel tasks. *Alberta Journal of Educational Research, 27.* 264-271.

Naylor, H. (1980). Reading Disability and lateral asymmetry: an information-processing analysis. *Psychological Bulletin, 87,* 531-545.

Oomen, C. (1973). India. In J. Downing (Edt.) *Comparative Reading.* New York: McMillan.

Ormrod, J. E., and Cochran, C.F. (1988). Relationship of verbal ability and working memory to spelling achievement and learning to spell. *Reading Research and Instruction, 28,* 33-43.

Padhi, B.B. (1971). *Bruhat Oriya Abhidhan,* Cuttack, Orissa, India: Friends' Publishers.

Patttanayak, D.P. (1985). *Oriya Bhasha O Bhasha Vigyan.* Cuttack Orissa, India : Granth Mandir.

Pattanayak, D.P. (1969). *Aspects of Applied Linguistics.* Bombay: Asia Publishing House.

Perfetti, C.A., and Lesgold, A.M. (1979). Coding and comprehension in skilled reading and implications for reading instruction. In L.B. Resnick and P.A. Weaver (Eds.). *Theory and Practice of Early Reading. Vol. I,* New Jersy : LEA Publishers.

Piaget, J. (1955). *The Language and Thought of the Child.* Meridian Books; Cleveland.

Potter, F.N. (1980). Miscue analysis: A coutionary note. *Journal of Research in Reading, 3,* 116-127.

Potter, F.N. (1981). Miscue analysis: some problems of interpretations and some possible solutions. *Journal of Research in Reading, 15,* 21-26.

Praharaj, G.C. (1936). *Purnachandra Oriya Bhashakosh,* Cuttack, Orissa, India : Utkal Sahitya Press.

Pratt, A.C., and Bradly. S. (1988). Relation of phonological awareness to reading disability in children and adults. *Journal of Educational Psychology, 80,* 319-323.

Ramey, G.W. (1985). The role of planning in reading comprehension. unpublished Ph. D. thesis, University of Alberta, Edmonton, Canada.

Raven, J.C. (1956). *Coloured Progressive Matrices: Sets-A Ab, B.,* London: H.K. Lewis.

Raven, J.C. (1962). *Coloured Progressive Matrices.* H.K.Lewis & Co. Ltd., : London.

Raven, J.C. (1965). *Guide to Using the Coloured Progressive Matrices,* London: H.K.Lewis.

Raz,I.S. and Bryant, P. (1990). Social background, phonological awareness and children's reading. *British Journal of Developmental Psychology, 8,* 209-225.

Reitsma, P. (1983). Word-specific knowledge in beginning reading. *Journal of Research in Reading, 6* (1), 41-56.

Reyner, K., and Pollatsek, A. (1989). *The Psychology of Reading.* New Jersy : Prentice-Hall.

Richman, L.C. & Lindgren, S.D. (1980). Patterns of intellectual ability in children with verbal deficits. *Journal of Abnormal Child Psychology, 8,* 65-81.

Ryckman, D.B. (1981). Reading achievement, IQ, and simultaneous successive processing among normal and learning disabled children. *Alberta Journal of Educational Research, 27,* 74-83.

Sahu, S. (1978). Psycholinguistic competence and language achievement of socially disadvantage at primary school level. Unpublished Ph. D. Thesis, Department of Psychology, Utkal University, Orissa.

Sahu, S., Patnaik, N., & Mishra, J. (1978). *Language Achievement Test Battery (for Grades-III, IV & V),* Department of Psychology, Utkal University, Bhubaneswar, India.

Sahu, S., Pattnaik, N., & Mishra, J. (1979). *Language Achivement Test Battery (for Grades-I & II),* Department of Psychology, Utkal University, Bhubaneswar, India.

Sahu, S. and Devi, G. (1984). Reading ability and information processing strategies. *Journal of Research in Reading, 7* (1), 33-40.

Sahu, S. and Devi, S. (1986). Information Processing strategies and

Beginning Reading. Unpublished M. Phil Thesis, Department of Psychology, Utkal University, Orissa.

Sahu, S. (1985). *Learning to Read: Use of Orthographic and Context Cues.* Meerut: Anu Books.

Sahu, S.; & Patnaik, S. (1987). Reading proficiency and strategies of disadvantaged children. *Psycho-lingua, 17 (1),* 39-54.

Sahu, S., and Mishra, A. (1988). Use of context cues in reading by socially advantaged and disadvantaged children. *Psycho-lingua,* 18, 117-128.

Sahu, S. and Mishra, S. (1993). Lexical access in Oriya orthography - The impact of suppression condition. Paper Presented in *First International Symposium on Multidisciplinary Prespectives on Cognition,* Banaras Hindu University, India.

Sahu, S., Mohanty, S. and Singh, S. (1995). Reflection impulsivity and reading in Oriya orthography. Invited Address at the *Second International Symposium on Cognition and Education,* Banaras Hindu University, Varanasi, India.

Schonell, F.J. & Schonell, F.E. (1955). *Schonell Reading Tests.* Edinburg : Oliver & Boyd.

Seigel, L.S. and Ryan, E.B. (1989). The development of working memory in normally achieving and subtypes of learning disabled children. *Child Development, 60,* 973-980.

Sgall, P. (1987). Towards a theory of phenomic orthography. In P. A. Lueldroff (Edt.) *Orthography and Phonology.* Amsterdam: John Benjamins Publishing Company.

Shallice, T. (1982). Specific impairments of planning. *Philosophical Transaction of the Royal Society of Londan, 298,* 199-209.

Smith, F. (1979). Conficting approaches to reading research and instruction. In L.B. Resnick and P.Weaver (Eds.) *Theory and Practice of Early Reading, Vol. II,* New Jersy: LEA Publishers.

Sousley, S. & Gargiulo, R. (1981). Effect of conceptual tempo on kindergarten reading readiness. *Perceptual and Motor Skills, 53,* 127-134.

Stevenson, H.W., Stigler, J.W., Lucker, W., Hsu, C., and Kitamura, S. (1982). Reading disabilities: The case of Chinese, Japanese and English. *Child Development, 53,* 1164-1181.

Taylor, I. (1981). Writing system and reading. In G.E. Mackinnon and T.G. Waller (Eds.) *Reading Research : Advances in Theory and Practice. Vol. II,* New York : Academic Press.

Torgsen, J.K., and Houck, D.G. (1980). Processing deficiencies of learning disabled children, who perform poorly on the digit span test. *Journal of Educational Psychology. 72,* 141-160.

Varshney, R.L. (1988). *An Introductory Text Book of Linguistics and Phonetics.* Student Store: Bareilly.

Vellutino, F.R. and Scanlon, D.M. (1982). Verbal processing in poor and normal readers. In C.J. Brainered and M.Pressley (Eds.), *Verbal Processes in Children: Progress in Congnitive Development Research,* Springler - Verlag; New York.

Vygotsky, L.S. (1962). *Thought and Language.* M.I.T. Press and John Willy and Sons: New York and London.

Vellutino, F.R., and Scanlon, D.M.(1987). Linguistic coding and reading ability. In S. Rosenberg (Ed.), *Advances in Applied Psycholinguistics,* Cambridge University Press: Cambridge.

Wagner,R.K., and Torgesen, J.K. (1987). The nature of phonological processing and its casual role in the acquisition of reading skill. *Psychological Bulletin, 101,* 192-212.

Walters, R.H., & Doan, H. (1962). Perceptual and cognitive functioning of retarded readers. *Journal of Consulting Psychology, 26,* 355-361.

Winer, B.J. (1971). *Statistical Principles in Experimental Design.* New York: McGraw Hill Book Company.

Yamada, J., Imai,H., & Ikebe, Y. (1990). The use of the orthographic lexicon in reading Kana words. *The Journal of General Psychology, 117,* 311-323.

Yamada, J.; Mitarai, Y.; and Yoshida, T. (1991). Kanji words are easier to indentify than katakana words. *Psychological Research, 53,* 136-141.

Zifcak, M. (1981). Phonological awareness and reading acquisition. *Contemporary Educational Psychology, 6,* 117-126.

INDEX